BRANDY

Edible

Series Editor: Andrew F. Smith

EDIBLE is a revolutionary new series of books dedicated to food and drink that explores the rich history of cuisine. Each book reveals the global history and culture of one type of food or beverage.

Already published

Brandy

A Global History

Becky Sue Epstein

REAKTION BOOKS

Published by Reaktion Books Ltd
33 Great Sutton Street
London EC1V 0DX, UK
www.reaktionbooks.co.uk

First published 2014

Printed and bound in China
by Toppan Printing Co. Ltd

A catalogue record for this book is available
from the British Library

ISBN 978 1 78023 348 2

Contents

Introduction:
Luxury Cognacs,
Alluring Brandies

No, sir, claret is the liquor for boys; port for men; but
he who aspires to be a hero (smiling), must drink brandy.
In the first place, the flavour of brandy is most grateful to
the palate; and then brandy will do soonest for a man what
drinking can do for him.

James Boswell, *The Life of Samuel Johnson* (1791)

Today, brandy is back in the limelight. It is cocktail chic. It is
a luxury sipping spirit in thousand-dollar crystal decanters. It
is the party drink of celebrities. Yet only a few decades ago,
brandy was far removed from this illustrious position.

Everyone knows what brandy is – or do they? Brandy is
a wonderful, aromatic spirit made by distilling wine. It is
usually amber- or mahogany-coloured as a result of its ageing
in wooden barrels. Today, the most famous brandies in the
United States and Britain are cognac and armagnac, which are
produced in two different regions of southern France.
Spanish and other brandies are also popular in various parts
of the world.

Until a few decades ago, expensive brandies were carefully measured out by the wealthy as after-dinner drinks. Older

people might keep a bottle of basic brandy at the back of a cupboard, for vaguely medicinal purposes. A certain amount of brandy was sold as cheap tipple. But for most of us, brandy simply wasn't part of our lives.

One bright spot remained: cognac, the most famous brandy in the world. Brandies from Cognac have always retained their cachet. When asked, most people have a favourable view of cognac even if they've never encountered it. Cognac is the most famous and expensive brandy, a concept reinforced again and again by today's stars. Legendary film director Martin Scorsese has been featured in adverts for Hennessy. The rap music star Ludacris has his own brand, Conjure; Snoop Dogg has endorsed Landy Cognac, and many other successful rappers mention favourite cognacs in their hit songs. In the current high-end bar scene, stylish bartenders (now called mixologists) compete in cognac cocktail contests, selecting subtle flavourings to create exceptional drink blends that enhance this elegant, aromatic spirit.

Technically, brandies can be distilled from a variety of fruits, but for the purpose of this book, brandy is defined as a spirit made from grape wine. The wine is distilled into a spirit, and then most often aged in wood, which gives brandy its lovely tawny colour. This is what we think of as 'brandy'.

While young brandies can inspire cocktails and relaxation, sipping an aged cognac or brandy is a truly memorable event. We experience a wonderful sense of ease and well-being when a fine spirit of 40 per cent alcohol courses through our bodies. (Medicinal? Perhaps.)

As late as the end of the twentieth century, when brandy's fortunes were in decline, it was cognac that sparked its resurgence. Until that time, upmarket brandy from Cognac was seen as a drink for prosperous older people – mainly men. Through the middle of the century, it was only considered acceptable for women to consume cognac in public in dishes like crêpes Suzette, which is dramatically flamed at the table with a brandy-based sauce. Around the world, less wealthy populations with brandy traditions sipped much less expensive brandies, most often lower-quality domestic brands made from grape wine (as well as other substances) but still called 'brandy' – or even 'cognac'. These highs and lows were continuations of brandy's long progression through civilization, a journey that began more than 700 years ago.

Beginning in the Middle Ages, brandy was prescribed medicinally for a vast number of ills and conditions. In the modern era, brandy also served as the basic ingredient for many of the punch drinks that were extremely popular in the eighteenth and nineteenth centuries in the United States and Britain. During the middle of the nineteenth century, brandy became the base spirit for the first-ever cocktail craze, which originated in the u.s.

Due to its exacting distillation process, brandy is not an inexpensive spirit to produce. Factor in years of barrel-ageing, and still more is added to the price of a bottle. Cognac, armagnac and brandy de Jerez are the three most famous – and expensive – noble Old World brandies. Early in their histories, South Africa and Australia established thriving brandy industries because they were colonial outposts of Britain and the Netherlands, where people traditionally consumed cognac. High-quality, grape-wine-based brandies have been made in Armenia, Georgia, the u.s. and other countries for over 100 years.

Since cognac was the most widely known luxury brandy, many countries modelled their production on that of the Cognac region. Most countries even went so far as to call their brandy 'cognac'. This gradually became an identity problem for France's cognac producers, an issue that they have been actively dealing with since brandy production surged across the globe in the late 1800s.

Also towards the end of the nineteenth century, the availability of fine cognac from France began to decrease due to the phylloxera epidemic that decimated European vineyards. By the beginning of the twentieth century, with cognac's high prices and constrained availability, whisky and other spirits replaced brandy in many fashionable cocktails. So brandy – and cognac in particular – became even further removed from the daily world of most consumers. This situation continued through the middle decades of the century, when countless scenes in books and films reinforced the image of snobbery associated with drinking brandy. The suave spy James Bond created a little stir in the brandy world in 1971; in the film *Diamonds are Forever* he briefly took cognac out of the drawing room and into the line of fire, literally, when he used

Towards the end of harvest time, Cognac's vineyards begin to fade from luscious green to the tans and ambers of cognac itself.

Courvoisier to flambé an opponent. But all in all, it appeared that brandies were being relegated to the increasingly rarely used drawing room.

Yet suddenly, at the turn of the twenty-first century, brandy – more specifically cognac – was dusted off and brought into the mainstream, largely through the genre known as urban music and the unlikely agency of rap and hip hop artists. During the latter decades of the twentieth century, lower-end brandies had been very popular in certain urban areas in the u.s. When urban music styles took off, even young people who didn't live in these areas began to emulate the lifestyle they heard on the radio and saw in videos. As the number of hip hop and rap stars increased, more mentions of luxury bottles of Courvoisier, Hennessy and other top brands began to show up in their songs and in their music videos. And fans followed enthusiastically into the world of luxury cognac. Abruptly, cognac consumption exploded.

At the same time, bartenders were also becoming more creative, turning into professional 'mixologists'; and cocktails were gaining in popularity in upmarket urban establishments. Though it may be impossible to proclaim either music or mixologists as the ultimate catalyst, the result is clear: brandy – and cognac in particular – is in the ascendancy again.

Today, in New York and other cosmopolitan cities, people are more likely to have their brandy before dinner than after. In the early evening behind the bar, cognac is often poured into a cocktail shaker. There, mixologists perform their magic by adding select flavourings and other liquors and liqueurs to turn it into the perfect, chilled cocktail. Increasingly, adventurous imbibers sample brandy for the first time this way: in a heady concoction at an upscale bar. This is especially true of cognac. Expensive cognac cocktails have taken off in major u.s. cities, and other urban areas around

Cognac Hardy recently created a series of cognacs in magnificent, sculptural glass carafes. As it happens, these cognacs echo the alchemical origins of cognac itself because they are named after the four elements in alchemy: earth, air, fire and water. Hardy have also added a fifth 'element', light.

the world are starting to follow this enticing lead, guided by internationally oriented mixologists.

For aged brandies, the UK and the U.S. have been the traditional leaders in consumption. But China is currently overtaking the West, after more than a decade of soaring consumption that shows no sign of abating. And there's still a huge market for basic brandies around the world; Malaysia, the Philippines, India and other Asian countries are all major brandy consumers. How can this spirit be popular on so many levels? And what are all these levels?

In addition to place of origin, ageing makes the most difference to the price and quality of brandies. But they all start with the same process: distillation. It has been a long journey, one that took centuries, as distillation moved from the centre of the ancient world to Europe and then to the New World. This is the story we will explore.

distillandi aquas.

QVINTA FORNAX.

Distillation device.

I

Alchemy: From Classical Civilizations to Cognac

Fire and gold, Dionysus and Cleopatra, early Christianity and secret sects all played a part in the history of distillation. Early distillers in classical civilizations had several different goals. Some were looking for an elixir of life, or *aqua vitae*. Others were also producing *aqua ardens*, the miraculous combination of two opposing elements, water and fire; *aqua ardens* was a magical 'burning water', an ignitable liquid. Later, in the early Middle Ages, alchemists created different types of distillates while seeking to create the highest of all metals, gold. Early Egyptians explored distillation as early as Cleopatra's reign in Egypt in the first century BC, when two slightly different types of distilling were practised by respected philosopher-chemists, and distilled wine was also used by Greek followers of the cult of Dionysus.

Though distilling seemed to have disappeared once the Roman Empire became Christian, in reality it only went underground. For centuries, the process was used to prepare fluids for the sacred rituals of secret Gnostic sects. During the course of a thousand years, religious Cathars underwent a true 'baptism by fire' involving 'burning water' (*aqua ardens*) which was created by distillation. The technique may also have spread to Asia – or developed simultaneously. Early Arab alchemists had apparently heard rumours that distillation was used by Taoists in China to create an 'elixir of life' (*aqua vitae*) in the fourth century. But in the West in the third century, even common sailors understood the concept of distilling; essentially they evaporated sea water and then carefully condensed it to obtain the desalinated water they desperately needed on long voyages. To them, this was the 'water of life', the *aqua vitae* that literally kept them alive.

It was only one more step to use the concept of distilling as a weapon. Warring sailors used *aqua ardens* at the Battle of Cyzicus, an island in the Sea of Marmara, around the year 672. There, Byzantines successfully defended the great city of Constantinople by throwing flaming liquid at the attacking Saracen ships. Though this 'Greek fire' may have involved petroleum in addition to (possibly instead of) distilled wine, it nevertheless became part of the lore of distillation's power, and the force of its resultant product, *aqua ardens*.

Knowledge of distillation also spread through the Middle East to the Persian Empire, where it was used to achieve more positive results in the emerging science of herbal medicine. In the sixth century, the Persian shah Khosrau I established a medical school in his city of Gundeshapur. Surrounding the academy were gardens filled with herbs, flowers and other botanical specimens. Distilling alcohol was critical here, as it was used to prepare all kinds of medicinal infusions.

Under the Moorish occupation, this non-drinking culture did not destroy Spain's existing vineyards, because grapes were also necessary for the distillation process to make perfumes and make-up. In fact, the word 'alcohol' is thought to come from the Arab word for the dark eyeliner known as kohl (*al* means 'the' or 'a' in Arabic, forming *al-kuhl*). The name 'alembic' for the type of still also came from Arabic, which in turn was derived from *ambix*, the Greek word for cup. The word 'alembic' is found in written French as far back as 1265.

In Europe, distilling was part of the process alchemists used to try to turn ordinary items into gold. In fact, one chemical process involving distillation gives certain items a gold-coloured coating; this seems to have been enough to encourage many more generations to try to develop the process to make real gold. In addition to being considered the most important metal, gold was believed to be a cure for various illnesses and conditions. (The modern German liqueur Goldwasser, 'gold water', is a reminder of this belief.)

As chemistry, alchemy and medicine became intertwined during the Middle Ages, distillation became part of all of these fields. By the late Middle Ages, distilling for medicinal preparations had spread throughout northern Europe and the British Isles, through alchemists and physicians. But the world was now ready for another use – shall we call it recreational?

However, the results of distilling wine were mixed in the early days. For instance, in order to sell more wine, German merchants distilled wine with additives that included poisonous chemicals. Many people attempted to distil matter other than grape wine, which had a variety of results, mostly bad. Eventually, this experimentation led to the production of whisky, which of course was good. But before that, we had brandy.

Drinkable brandy was reliably produced by distilling grape wine. One of the first commercial uses of potable brandy – at the time a clear, un-aged spirit – was to fortify existing wine. A spirit can be added to wine to stabilize it against spoilage by strengthening its alcohol content. Sometimes, to create a sweeter wine, the spirit is added during fermentation, which kills the yeast before it can convert all the grape sugars into alcohol. The great sweet wines of Roussillon

Alchemical symbols included the four basic elements: earth, air, water and fire. Alchemists often exhibited their prowess in controlling the elements as well as employing highly symbolic animals such as these snakelike dragons.

from the Mediterranean coast of France are still fortified with locally distilled spirits today.

The science of distilling had moved further north into the Gascony area of France by the thirteenth century, perhaps brought by pilgrims returning from Santiago de Compostela. And in 1299, we have evidence that Arnaud de Villeneuve, the private physician of Pope Clement V, was treating him with medicine made from distilled grape wine. He called it the water of life, *aqua vitae* in Latin; in French it was *eau de vie*, which remains the common French term for a distilled spirit to this day.

A short time later, in Armagnac (located in Gascony) we find this wine-grape distillate being stored (aged) in barrels, thus launching the modern era of brandy. It was the Armagnac region that gave its name to the first aged brandies in 1310, just over 700 years ago. From Gascony, brandy distillation spread further: south to the Andalusian region of Spain where the town of Jerez is located – Jerez is not only the home of sherry but also of the great brandy de Jerez – and north along the Atlantic coast of France, to Bordeaux, Cognac and the Loire Valley.

Dutch traders sailed up and down the Atlantic coast of Europe from the early sixteenth century. In particular, they brought home wines from France because it was too cold to grow wine grapes in Holland. Contrary to what is written in most short histories of brandy, there was no instant, meteoric rise in the dissemination of distilled spirits from Cognac. In fact, Dutch traders took their wines from towns along the rivers that fed into the Atlantic coast of western France. Perhaps initially Dutch traders distilled some of the weaker wines in order to stabilize them for the journey home, or perhaps it was simply more efficient to ship concentrated, distilled wine; this was first called *brandewijn* (cooked or 'burned' wine), a term which was later shortened to *brandy*.

The Dutch drank brandy from at least the year 1536; this is documented in a regulation which prohibited tavern-keepers from selling brandy to be consumed off their premises. Britain imported brandy for householders to make cordials, to 'strengthen' weak wines and to provide a base for medicinal herbs and spices. But British, French and Dutch business dealings in cognac were severely interrupted by the Glorious Revolution and the Nine Years' War at the end of the seventeenth century. Of course, a brisk trade immediately grew up in counterfeit brandy – distillations made with all sorts of fruits and spices that attempted to mimic the French drink's flavours.

Dutch ships were extraordinarily seaworthy, plying the waters of the Atlantic Coast of Europe; this one is riding high in the water, making good time on the way to pick up goods, like distilled wines from the Cognac region, to take back to eager customers in Holland.

Smuggling was another 'industry' that benefited from the politics of the seventeenth and eighteenth centuries. Even at times when there was no ongoing war, there was a plentiful market for brandies that had evaded British taxes by being put ashore on the many inlets along the English coastline. The Irish gentry drank brandy, too, and they even sent some of their merchants to Cognac to run operations there – which is why some of the most famous cognac houses today have Irish names, like Hennessy and Otard (originally O'Tard).

In Europe, Britain and America, brandy was considered medicinal, and in most households it was kept as a remedy for everything from fainting to indigestion. Travellers carried it for energy and as an antiseptic. 'Medicinal brandy' is a phrase many people today have heard – or used – without knowing exactly what it meant. Whether considered a necessity of life or a recreational beverage, the distilled grape wine called brandy has been a staple commodity throughout the Western world for the past several centuries.

2
Producing Brandy: Distilling and Ageing

Everyone knows brandy is a golden-brown spirit. Or is it? Most consumers – even connoisseurs – are not familiar with brandy's method of production. In fact, brandy starts out clear. Most brandies are aged in wood, which imparts a lovely amber hue to the clear liquid that deepens over time. But whether clear or coloured, the spirit is still brandy. In fact, one of the newly popular spirits in Western mixology is a clear brandy called pisco. Yes, pisco, which originated in Peru, is a brandy. It's made in the same way as cognac from France and brandy de Jerez from Spain: distilled from grape wine. But it isn't generally aged in oak barrels, hence its clear colour.

Grape-wine-based brandy, which is the focus of this book, is one of three main types of brandy. The others are distilled from other fruits and from pomace. Well-known brandies made from fruit include calvados (apples), slivovitz (plums) and kirsch (cherries), but there are many more national and local favourites around the globe. Pomace-based brandies are distilled from the skins, stems and seeds of wine grapes – the leftovers after the grapes have been pressed for wine. Two of the most famous pomace brandies are grappa from Italy and marc, a name that originated in France. Why are we not

Distilled as a colourless liquid, brandy gains its rich golden and amber hues as it matures in wooden barrels.

talking about fruit and pomace brandies in this book? Because most people don't think of spirits like grappa as brandies. And there are so many amazing grape-based brandies around the world.

What all three categories of brandy have in common is that they are made by distillation. Distillation is what turns them from their raw material – grapes, fruit, pomace – into a spirit. Recalling the history of distillation, it was a process used by alchemists in the Middle Ages before brandies started to become well-known, tradable commodities. Perhaps it's no accident that the word 'spirit' refers to a substance or essence that is vital and strong, both in the context of alcohol and in the disciplines of philosophy and religion. Having discovered earlier how distilling made its way from the Middle East into Europe, it will be interesting to see how this process is used in the production of brandy in various regions.

Very simply, distillation is the process of heating wine in a closed container, then capturing the resultant aromatic, alcoholic vapour, and cooling it into a liquid. The wine is heated to its boiling point, a temperature at which more alcohol than water evaporates. (Alcohol boils at 78°C (172°F), while water's boiling temperature is 100°C (212°F).) The alcohol is concentrated in the resulting condensed liquid: this is when wine becomes a spirit. And some of the wine's aromas and flavours are carried in the alcohol as it evaporates and then condenses, which gives each brandy its own distinct character.

Of course, brandy distilling is not quite as simple as boiling up a wine; if it was, anyone would be able to do it. In reality, it can be quite a complex, beautiful process, with a bright copper vessel shining like a giant kettle in a large room redolent of wood smoke from the fires underneath. The huge copper pot is connected to other containers with angled, columnar or even corkscrew-shaped pipes, so that the whole collection looks like a massive, playfully gleaming laboratory apparatus – especially pleasing when you consider the wonderful product being created.

Three main factors influence the creation of brandy: the type of wine, the type of distilling equipment and the skill of the distiller. Each brandy region also has its own set of regulations and traditions that contribute to the final product. These include elements such as the type of still that may be used, which months of the year distilling must take place in, the ageing process and the shapes of the bottles.

Most of the wines used to make brandy are made from white grapes that have two properties. First, they have good acidic components. Second, the grapes are capable of imparting desirable aromas and flavours to a brandy after distillation. Traditionally, grapes used for brandy did not make great wines – though that is not universally true.

After the grapes are harvested, they are fermented into wine. It is important that the wine is distilled immediately (unless it can be held in a temperature-controlled environment) because the common wine preservative sulphur dioxide (SO_2) would effectively ruin the distilled spirit. Historically, this is why Cognac and Armagnac dictated that wine distilling had to start on a certain day (just after the grapes had been fully fermented into wine) and finish by the end of the winter, when the weather was still cold enough to preserve the wine naturally. Nowadays, wines can be held in chilled tanks for weeks or months until they are ready to be distilled, but the tradition endures in the rules set by the regions.

Most commonly, wine is taken off the lees – the dregs of the yeast and other residue in the wine that settles during fermentation – before it is distilled, as it is easy for the lees to fall to the bottom of the still and burn, ruining a batch of brandy. However, those producers who do distil with the lees say it makes a more flavourful drink, worth the extra effort of installing a propeller-type mixer in the still to keep the lees circulating in the wine.

The distillation process of an entire vintage of wine can take several months, since there is generally a limited number of stills – and expert distillers – available at any given facility. In the world of brandies, there are basically two types of distilling process: single distillation and double distillation. Because multiple distillations are currently being popularized in the vodka world, you might think that more is better. In brandy, it's not. Ask anyone from Armagnac, where single distillation is the honoured tradition. But move to Cognac, and you might think that double distillation is the only way to go.

Both distillation processes produce many impurities, from foul aromas or terrible flavours like fusel oil (which tastes more like something you'd use in an engine than a drink) to downright dangerous chemicals. 'Heads' are compounds that are more volatile than ethanol, meaning that they evaporate and condense at a lower temperature than ethanol; 'tails' are compounds less volatile than ethanol, and evaporate and condense at higher temperatures. During double distillation, heads and tails are typically discarded at the beginning and end of the second distillation. Double distillation is practised in Cognac as well as in some other regions. The wine literally goes through the process of distilling twice; sometimes parts of the heads or tails are added into the second distillation, sometimes not, depending on the company's tradition and the master distiller's style.

Devotees of the single-distillation process – such as those in Armagnac and Jerez – will tell you that this is a far more exacting process than double distilling. In single distillation, the temperature gradient of the distillation column separates the heads and tails from the desirable spirit. The master distiller

Armagnac's distillation process traditionally takes place in columnar stills, sometimes small enough to be carried from farm to farm on wagons.

must carefully manage the temperature and operation of the column still in order to remove the undesirable compounds and to keep all of the desirable aromas and flavours and the degree of alcohol in a single process.

Many distillers use gas heat, but some distilleries use wood fires to heat their stills. At Château du Tariquet in

Armagnac – as well as a few others in this region, and in Cognac and Jerez – the smoky aromas greatly enhance the experience for lucky visitors during the autumn distillation period.

After distillation, the finished spirit is ready to be aged. The wood-ageing process contributes enticing aromas ranging from vanilla and toffee to dried fruits, cedar and spices. In most regions, towards the end of the ageing period, a certain amount of carefully filtered water must usually be added to dilute the brandy to its final drinking strength, which is around 40 per cent alcohol. 'Cask strength' (the alcohol content straight out

Noble Spanish brandies – brandy de Jerez – are made in the same traditional manner as Cognac's. Here are some of the old, well-used copper pot stills in the Gonzalez-Byass distillery in Jerez, Spain.

of the barrel) is for most brandies around 60 to 70 per cent – though this level changes over the years as both alcohol and water evaporate (at different rates) during the ageing process.

Every region has a preferred wood that it uses to make the barrels for ageing its brandies. Limousin oak, from near Cognac, is considered the gold standard, but there are other forests of oaks with a similar grain in Armagnac, the Caucasus Mountains and elsewhere. Some brandy producers actually go to the forest to choose the trees to use for barrels, while others may select already cut wood at their cooperage. Wood for the ageing barrels must be left out to air-dry for several years.

Most of the barrels for cognac and other high-end brandies are handmade. First the dried staves are heated gently to make them flexible, and then they are assembled like a giant upside-down flower around a small fire. In Cognac, this is called *mise en rose*, or putting it into a rose-shape. Bands are then placed on top and slowly hammered down into place, holding the staves together. After a barrel's inside is 'toasted' to order, the ends are added, and the finished barrel is rolled out of the hot, smoky work area, as has been done for hundreds of years.

Barrel-ageing rooms are dark and quiet and may be above ground or below. As brandies develop, they may be moved from warmer to cooler, or from more to less humid areas. Originally, small producers kept their barrels in their farm out-buildings, and many still do today, while large cognac houses age barrels in their cellars or in other types of warehouses.

But in Cognac, all the ageing rooms have one thing in common: spiders. It is bad luck to kill the spiders. Until very recently, cognac was aged in barrels held together with willow bands, because willow is flexible. However, there is a certain type of mite in Cognac that likes to eat willow wood. The spiders are there to eat the mites, thus keeping the cognac barrels intact for decades, so cognac producers take care not

A barrel-ageing *chai* or cellar in Cognac may not be underground. It may be a stone barn on a small farm, where the air is rarely disturbed and spiders guard the barrels while the cognacs mature.

to disturb them. Even now, when most barrels are bound with metal bands, there is still a superstition that a healthy cellar must contain plenty of spiders – perhaps a far cry from the luxurious image of this spirit, yet essential.

3
Cognac becomes World-famous

It is impossible to tour the small art museum in the city of Cognac without noticing that the man who was king of France 500 years ago – Francis I – tends to be smiling in his portraits and statues. And he had every reason to be happy. During his reign, the riverside town of Cognac was already well known as a shipping centre in the region, and the brandy business was just beginning. Dutch merchants were expanding their reach in the area, looking for new products to trade.

The most pervasive theory about the 'invention' of cognac has to do with Dutch traders fortifying the local wine for shipping, only to reconstitute it with water on arrival in their home cities. But this is a simplification of what really happened. Dutch merchants were the savviest traders of their era. They had a single-mindedness of vision: they knew what to buy and what to sell, what to build and how to do it, in order to maximize their profit. They traded tirelessly along the Atlantic coast of France from the sixteenth century on. One of the more important commodities they brought to the Netherlands was the salt from the French coastal trading port of La Rochelle. La Rochelle sits just across a narrow channel from the Île de Ré – which is still famous today for its excellent-quality salt. The city also happens to be located very near the mouth of the Charente, the river that runs through Cognac. And, of course, there was the wine.

The winemakers of the Loire Valley shipped their wines to a merchant colony the Dutch had set up in the large trading city of Nantes on the Loire river, on the way to the Atlantic. The Dutch set up another colony further south, in the Charente river region. They also traded with Bordeaux, which was an easy trip along the Gironde estuary from the Atlantic.

Because some of these French wines could be fairly light in flavour and chemically fragile, traders sought a way to stabilize them for transportation. They also wanted to improve the wines' ageing potential, though not in the way we think of today, of ageing bottles of wine for years until the flavours mature. In those days, wine had to age only well enough to last out the year without spoiling, until the next year's grapes were harvested and made into wine.

But the wines from the Loire and from Bordeaux proved to be more valuable when sold as wines than as distilled spirits. So while the Dutch continued to import and sell the wines from the Loire and Bordeaux, they kept on distilling wines from the Cognac area because they were more profitable.

This was also a century of political and religious upheaval, which had its effects on the cognac trade. Wars and conflicts between the English and the French continued. Catholics and Protestants tangled in local, national and international clashes in France, England, Holland and other northern European countries.

One important local battle that occurred in the seventeenth century greatly impacted Cognac's rise to economic dominance in the region. During a battle in 1651, the people of the walled city of Cognac succeeded in holding back forces hostile to the Bourbon prince Louis II, who was a general in Louis xiv's army. In gratitude, King Louis later exempted Cognac from taxes and duties on its wines and distilled wines. With this financial advantage, Cognac soon began to outstrip its neighbours in economic development, becoming a regional commercial centre for all locally exported products – which included its brandy. Cognac was on its way to becoming the most famous brandy in the world.

Additional European and British political strife continued into the eighteenth century. Some Englishmen came to the Charente area to establish their own cognac production houses, so as not to be dependent on the French for a favourite – and quite profitable – spirit. Periodic Anglo-French conflicts also allowed the Irish to get into the cognac industry.

As this happened, the Dutch merchants lost their near-monopoly on the French brandy trade. Dutch citizens continued to crave spirits, but by then brandy was not the only one available to them. Developments in distilling had allowed people who lived in northern countries to create spirits from grain in places like Holland where it was too cold to grow wine grapes.

All these spirits, including brandy, were initially referred to as *eaux de vie*. But they soon acquired their own designated names, taken either from the local language or place where they were made. The Dutch had genever (or jenever; an early version of gin); the Scottish were starting to make Scotch whisky; Russia and other northern European countries began to produce vodkas; and rum arrived from the New World. But at the higher levels of society, the people of all these countries still enjoyed their cognac – especially in Holland, Germany and England. French, English and Irish names began to appear on the fronts of cognac houses in the first half of the eighteenth century. Some of these are still the top cognac producers today – names like Martell, Hennessy and Rémy Martin.

As this was happening, cognac began to differentiate itself from the other northern European spirits (or *eaux de vie*). Yes, they were all ardent, life-enhancing spirits, descended from a combination of alchemical, medical and religious practices. But cognac was a bit smoother, a little more refined – and more flavourful than other *eaux de vie* that existed at that time.

Several more elements aligned to contribute to cognac's quality and fame. One was the proximity of the Limousin forests, the source of wood for excellent cognac-ageing barrels. Another was cognac's period of popularity in Paris – and subsequently in French colonies around the globe. By the early eighteenth century residents of the north of France had become more aware of cognac. Unlike the English, they did not limit their consumption to high-end sipping; instead, they began to drink basic cognacs during the years when weather extremes caused problems in the vineyards and made local wines scarce. In fact, cognac has always had less cachet in France than in other countries, partly because of this early use of cognac, and partly because cognac was mainly considered an export product.

In order to be exported, cognac had to be put into barrels, made, of course, from local wood. The forests around the cognac production area were well known even in the Middle Ages. Later, their wood was used by Louis xiv's navy. This Limousin oak is considered top-quality even today. In Limousin oak (English oak or French oak, *Quercus robur*), cognac ages perfectly; the relatively loose wood grain of these trees allows just the right amount of liquid penetration inside the barrels, which transfers the ideal amounts of colour, spicy aroma and flavour from barrel to spirit.

The amber hues of cognac aged in barrels further distinguished cognac from *eaux de vie* that were produced from other fruits and grains at the same time. Those other spirits tended to be consumed in their local areas, and without barrel ageing they were clear in colour. Soon, barrel ageing became such a defining feature of the spirits from Cognac (as in Armagnac) that producers mastered the art of barrel construction and management solely for the enhancement of their cognacs.

As barrel ageing became an important characteristic of cognac, the concept of ageing itself took on new meaning. This is how the term 'Napoleon cognac' developed. At present, Napoleon cognac has a specific ageing requirement in the laws of Cognac, but this specificity is an only relatively recent development in Cognac, and is not generally adhered to around the world.

The motto of the famous Courvoisier cognac house is 'Le Cognac de Napoleon'. Courvoisier began as a wine and spirits company on the outskirts of Paris, which Napoleon Bonaparte is said to have visited in 1810. Perhaps because of this, he began issuing morning cognac rations to hearten his troops during the long Napoleonic Wars. Courvoisier was proud to advertise its connection with the emperor. Some years later, in 1828, after deciding to concentrate on cognac, Courvoisier relocated its company headquarters to the Cognac region. To this day Courvoisier headquarters remain there, in the town of Jarnac, on the Charente river just upstream from Cognac.

Some claim that Napoleon's advocacy of cognac was the reason many more brandy producers (in Cognac and in other areas of the world) began to name their cognac after the emperor. Others believe that the status of an aged cognac became a more important factor as the nineteenth century progressed, so the term 'Napoleon cognac' was used by more producers to designate valuable cognac that had, allegedly, been aged since the time of Napoleon. In any case, the name Napoleon served to increase both the cachet and the sales of

Traditional cognac barrels are bound with willow bands.

cognac – so much so that it was often appropriated for other brandies in other countries, which is a problem Cognac's producers are still dealing with today.

As the era of cognac's importance unfolded, in Britain cognac overcame a challenging protectionist tax when Prime Minister Robert Peel cut cognac tariffs by nearly a third in the 1840s. This was followed by a further tax reduction in 1860, and six years after that cognac shipments to Britain had doubled.

In Britain, it was common for some distributors to ship young cognacs in barrels direct from Cognac, and then age them in dockside warehouses. After bottling, the cognacs might be labelled with the name of the trusted merchant, and not that of the cognac producer. These cognacs were called 'early landed' and had a slightly different taste and aroma profile because they were aged in a climate different from Cognac's.

In America by that time brandy (usually cognac) had become extremely popular as the basis for cocktails. This was during the (first ever) cocktail craze, which lasted through most of the nineteenth century. In France, cognac also got its first bottling factory, so that customers could identify and appreciate the tawny colour of this unique spirit when it was shipped in glass bottles instead of barrels. Everything was going swimmingly for cognac until the end of the nineteenth century, when it all came crashing down.

In the United States, cognac had been the spirit of wealthy men throughout the country, notably in the South. But after the Civil War (1861–5) much of the Southern economy was ruined, and that market for cognac dried up. Americans had also begun producing their own whiskey, and the country developed a taste for its native spirits such as bourbon and rye. In addition, cheap rum was now available in the u.s. Towards the end of the nineteenth century these spirits started to replace cognac in the American lifestyle, not only in cocktails.

About the same time – in 1872, to be specific – a plague hit the vineyards of Cognac. It happened just as a new tax on wine and spirits was put in place to fund mandated remuneration after Napoleon iii lost the war with Prussia; with the addition of this tax, French domestic consumption of cognac declined drastically.

The ailment in the Cognac vineyards was a slow-growing pestilence; it took a good twenty years to destroy the vineyards.

The name of the killer was phylloxera, the grapevine-destroying louse that spread throughout Europe and decimated vineyards from the late nineteenth century into the early twentieth. No grapes in France were safe, and there was no cure, no way to destroy this ravenous pest. In Cognac, phylloxera spread slowly, over the course of several decades, eventually slashing the vineyards to a fraction of their size by the early 1890s.

True cognac is unique in the world because of its grapes and the region's climate, and in the experience of the people who distil and age it – and promote it, too. But to add to their misery, Cognac's producers found that demand for their high-quality spirits had inspired people in a variety of countries around the world to produce their own brandies. Many produced inferior spirits and labelled them 'cognac'. For example, producers in both Armenia and Georgia imported stills and knowledge from Cognac in the 1870s in order to produce high-quality 'cognac' for their domestic market. In the 1880s producers in Italy and Greece began marketing their domestic brandies widely. They used different grapes, and their products may (or may not) have been very good quality, but they all hijacked the name 'cognac' to sell their spirits. So, in addition to having to figure out how to reconstruct their vineyards, the people of Cognac had to learn how to compete with other brandies in the world market. And they had to begin the difficult process of challenging foreign producers in order to defend the uniqueness of the name and identity of cognac across the globe.

Back in Cognac, without an effective, long-term treatment for phylloxera, there was only one thing to do in the late 1800s: begin wholesale replacement of the vineyards with phylloxera-resistant vines. This is the 'cure' that was finally discovered, after everything from religious to chemical to water therapies (flooding the vineyards) had been tried.

As in the rest of France, Cognac planted rootstocks imported from America, and grafted European grapes on to the roots. This worked well in Bordeaux and Burgundy with grapes like Merlot, Cabernet Sauvignon and Pinot Noir. At first Cognac's growers grafted the same white grapes they had been using to make cognac for centuries: Folle Blanche and Colombard. But they found that Folle Blanche did not do as well on American rootstock, so they began to graft more

During the winter grapevines are neatly pruned, awaiting the next growing season.

and more vines with another white grape from the area, Ugni Blanc (also known as Trebbiano). Ugni Blanc made a slightly different, perhaps more undistinguished wine than Folle Blanche, but it distilled into a wonderful cognac – either with or without the addition of Colombard. Finally, Cognac would be able to get on with its grape growing and cognac production.

4
Armagnac and its Noble History

It seems fitting that today, the Armagnac region of central, southwest France has a timeless feel, the bucolic landscape looking much the same as it did hundreds of years ago. Armagnac is the most ancient brandy-producing area – older than Cognac by hundreds of years. The distilled spirit known as armagnac celebrated its 700th birthday not too long ago, in 2010. Why did distilling develop in Armagnac so early? And why didn't armagnac become more well known than cognac? The reasons for this are rooted in the region's geography.

Most armagnac houses have their production headquarters set in the countryside, with its rolling hills, small farms and pocket-sized pastures. They might be located near a village or out in the midst of their vineyards. A few producers are located in town centres, such as the Ryst Dupeyron armagnac cellars, which have been headquartered in the historic town of Condom for over 100 years. But what happened between the creation of armagnac in the 1300s and now? And how was armagnac initially created?

As described in chapter One, during the early Middle Ages the technique of distilling spread from the Middle East through the Iberian peninsula into the south of France. At that time, the Western world was in the process of a slow shift

Well-pruned vineyards at Chateau du Tariquet follow the contours of the rolling hills of Armagnac's enchanting landscape.

from the reign of magic and mystery to the ascendancy of science. Medicine straddled both fields, and doctors prescribed the wine distillate known as brandy, medicinally.

The first person to codify the health attributes of the distillations of armagnac in print was a Franciscan friar named Vital du Four, who lived from 1260 to 1327. Du Four wrote a medical book in 1310 relating the importance of Armagnac's distilled spirit to physical health – and this was the beginning of armagnac's fame. He called this spirit '*Aguay Ardente*' (*aqua ardente*) and it is considered the direct ancestor of the armagnac of today.

Du Four's work was so important that it was kept alive in manuscript form for centuries. With the invention of the printing press, it reached a still-wider audience. Vatican archives now house a copy of Du Four's book published in 1531. In his writings Du Four lists 42 benefits of consuming a drink made with Armagnac's *aqua ardente*. The miraculous properties include

The house at Château l'Aubade has been a feature in the Armagnac countryside since the early 20th century, when its brandies became well-known.

Today, the colourful facade of the historic house brightens the bucolic surroundings of Château l'Aubade.

curing wounds and sores; restoring memory; healing paralysed limbs; and imparting courage to the faint of heart.

Armagnac's production grew over the following centuries, keeping up with increasing demand in this part of France's Gascony region, whose landlocked geography played a major part in armagnac's development. In fact, the lack of commercially navigable rivers kept Armagnac relatively isolated from the outside world. So, though armagnac may claim to be the first French brandy of quality, until comparatively recently it was so difficult to export this spirit that it never became as famous as cognac worldwide.

Armagnac now differs from cognac in another significant way: it is manufactured in a single-distillation process. Though armagnac was initially produced in both single- and double-distilled pot stills, for the past two centuries it has consistently

A traditional armagnac columnar alembic still in use at Château du Tariquet, heated with a wood fire.

been made in the 'Alembic Armagnaçaise', a single squat, cylindrical still patented in 1818. This produces a fine brandy with an entirely different flavour profile from that of cognac.

This artisanal type of single distillation has another great advantage: it can be done in a still so small that it is portable. And this is what occurred in Armagnac: stills on wheels were moved from one small grape-grower to the next, allowing even ordinary farmers to make their own armagnac on their own land. The custom persists today and this, along with the slow growth of armagnac production in the past, has allowed many modestly sized producers to flourish among their vineyards. Artisanal producers on country lanes now add immensely to the charm of the region.

However, the grapes that armagnac is made from today are not the same as those that were used there until the late nineteenth century. As in the rest of France, Armagnac's vineyards suffered greatly during the phylloxera epidemic. Before phylloxera came to attack the roots and destroy all the *Vitis vinifera* (wine grape) plants, the highly acidic white grape Folle Blanche was the basis for armagnac, as it was for cognac. When the vineyard plague hit, a French breeder named François Baco developed a resistant grape that was a cross of the traditional Armagnac and Cognac grape Folle Blanche and an American grape called Noah (which had phylloxera-resistant roots). Now many producers find that this grape, with the unromantic name Baco 22A, makes the finest armagnacs – especially when planted on the sandy, gravelly soil of the best Bas-Armagnac areas.

Armagnac contains three regions, defined for the purposes of grape growing as well as production. Running basically west to east, Bas-Armagnac is considered the finest, then Armagnac-Ténarèze, then Haut-Armagnac. Today, Baco, Colombard, Folle Blanche and Ugni Blanc are the main grapes

Ugni Blanc grapes are critical in the production of both cognac and armagnac; this photo is from Armagnac Delord.

used in Armagnac. A total of ten grape varieties are allowed; the other six are the much less well known Clairette, Graisse, Jurançon Blanc, Mauzac (Blanc and Rosé) and Meslier-Saint-François.

As a spirit, armagnac tends to be fruitier and more floral than cognac. It also takes more time for armagnac's internal elements to meld together and soften with age, which means that even the entry-level tier of fine, smooth armagnac is often older than first-tier cognac, and consequently more expensive.

Though sometimes armagnac is aged in Limousin oak barrels from the forest near Cognac, when armagnac is put

Brandy producers secure their decades of mature brandies in a treasure room called the *paradis* (for obvious reasons); this one is at Armagnac Delord.

Demijohns of mature armagnac await their turn to be included in specially blended releases in the *paradis* treasury at Château l'Aubade.

into barrels from its native Gascon forests, it gains a different flavour profile and an increasingly golden tint throughout its life. Armagnac today has a tiered system of ageing, with rigorously enforced regulations. However, the Bureau National Interprofessionnel de l'Armagnac (BNIA, established in 1941) is in the process of simplifying the descriptive terms for armagnac labelling. It advocates the following standards: the entry level, VS or 3-star, is defined as having had over one year of ageing; mid-range VSOP must be over four years old; Hors d'âge denotes a true, aged armagnac at least ten years old, with the age also given on the label (for example ten, fifteen, twenty-five years); and Vintage armagnacs must be at least ten years old and must list the year of harvest on their labels. The Bureau also wants to see categories which are used to grade cognacs, such as XO, Vieux and Napoléon, being phased out in Armagnac.

After bottling, armagnac is ready to drink; it does not improve in the bottle. But once opened, it keeps for many weeks, even months, when stored in a cool place. Currently, up to 500 producers and 300 cooperatives produce a total of about 6 million bottles of armagnac a year. Major labels on the shelves in the U.S. and UK include Baron de Sigognac, Castarède, Darroze, Dartigalongue, Delord, Gélas, Janneau, Laubade, Larressingle, Marquis de Montesquiou, Pellehaut, Ryst Dupeyron, Samalens and Tariquet.

While it remains a relatively rare spirit in the U.S. (a bit less rare in the UK), armagnac's popularity is on the ascendancy in China. With modern transportation, the spirit is now unhindered by the geographical constraints of trade that limited its distribution for centuries. As a prestige spirit in East Asia, armagnac satisfies a desire for full flavour in a drink and carries

previous: The beautifully designed, modern barrel-ageing cellar at armagnac producer Marquis de Montesquiou.

Different styles of armagnac bottles are distinguished by hand-dipped, brightly coloured wax tops at Armagnac Delord.

Justly proud of their mature brandies, some producers show them off in a gallery, as at Château l'Aubade in Armagnac.

In keeping with tradition, certain armagnac labels are handwritten and hand-finished on the bottles.

After the armagnac bottles have been filled, each is hand-stamped with the insignia of the house at Armagnac Delord. This is a special bottle with armagnac that is over half a century old.

the status of a long history, as well as being presented in appealingly sophisticated packaging. Armagnac has taken off meteorically in China in the course of only a few years; by 2012 China's consumption of armagnac exceeded that of the u.s.

5
Illustrious Brandies of Europe and the Caucasus

As the illustrious reputation of cognac spread during the nineteenth century, it inspired brandy production in other countries in Europe and further east, notably Armenia and Georgia in the Caucasus Mountains.

In the late nineteenth century, distillers could trade on the fame of cognac, making brandy that was less expensive to produce and that sold for much less than imported cognac. In many areas, the local brandies were even called 'cognac', a term that has been slowly transitioning to 'brandy' around the world after much hard campaigning by cognac producers. Outside Cognac, most brandy manufacturers made their spirits with local grapes, but some imported stills, techniques and even grapes from Cognac.

In Germany, for example, where cognac carried a significant reputation, many brandy producers imported some or all of their brandy grapes from Cognac. Even today, top German brandy producers Asbach Uralt and Dujardin bring in grapes from the Charente (Cognac) region – as do some brandy producers as far away as Asia, including Russia and India.

In Italy, brandy has been distilled since the sixteenth century, but the country does not have a designated geographic region for brandy production. One of Italy's most distinguished brandy companies has been around since 1820 when a Cognac native called Jean Bouton found his way to Emilia Romagna and discovered Cognac's Ugni Blanc grapes (known as Trebbiano) were grown there as well. He became known as 'Giovanni Buton' when he established his distillery and began producing Vecchia Romagna brandy – which remains one of the top-selling Italian brands today. Stock, an Italian brandy producer established in 1884, makes some of the best-known brandies in Europe. Though its heyday was in the 1960s and 1970s, it is still extremely popular in Italy and other countries.

Another top Italian commercial brandy is made by Fratelli Branca, whose Stravecchio Branca brandy is a household name; a common Italian recipe for a sore throat treatment is a dollop of this brandy in a glass of hot milk. The company began making brandy in 1888, with a unique process: before bottling, Fratelli Branca blends in up to two-thirds of an existing brandy which is kept ageing in a 'mother barrel', so their finished blends contain brandies aged for anywhere from three to ten years. Fratelli Branca also produces a premium distilled brandy called Magnamater. Other Italian companies produce high-end products aimed at connoisseurs, as well: wine- and grappa-producing companies that also make brandies include Villa Zarri, Marchesi de' Bianchi and Giori, and the winemaker Marchese Antinori, the sparkling winery Bellavista and grappa producer Jacopo Poli.

Moving across the Mediterranean to Greece, we find an interesting aside in the most famous Greek 'brandy', Metaxa. (This is a drink many travellers have intense memories of, from youthful Mediterranean holidays.) Spyros Metaxa began producing his eponymous spirits in 1888, and Metaxa's fame has spread around the world. His spirits were a welcome departure from the harsh, local product of their time. However, he

A postage stamp issued in 2007 commemorates Nikolay Shustov, considered the father of the important Armenian brandy industry.

combined his distillate with sweet muscat wine and herbs, so strictly speaking, classic Metaxa is not a (classic) brandy.

Further east, quality brandies are also produced in the Caucasus, in Armenia and Georgia. Long hidden from Western view, first by geographical remoteness and then by the Iron Curtain, these countries have prolific brandy companies with long traditions of quality brandies made with Charentais (Cognac-style) distillation and ageing, which they supplied to the tsars of Russia. Legend has it that when the Bolsheviks breached the Winter Palace in 1917, the entire revolution paused for a week while the revolutionaries drank up the Tsar's incredible brandies.

Until a couple of decades ago, Armenia was the main designated producer of brandies supplied to Russia and other countries of the Soviet Union. When the USSR was disbanded, distribution networks disappeared overnight and the market

Quality brandies have been produced in Yerevan, Armenia, for over a century, as these bottles and barrels attest.

The Yerevan Brandy Company's cellars are full of star power, with aisles that commemorate famous Armenians and barrels signed by celebrities and politicians.

for Armenian brandy collapsed. Currently, the Armenian industry is rebuilding itself; its former markets have stabilized and its producers are looking towards new markets.

Today there are three large brandy-producing companies in Armenia, and some struggling with privatization. A few are still located in the capital city of Yerevan, generally with updated facilities. Others are located on the surrounding, high, arid plateaux of this mountainous country. The major companies are Ararat, Noy and Proshyan, with other producers such as the formerly-great Vedi-Alco at the start of a comeback.

Confusingly, both Ararat and Noy are sometimes referred to as the Yerevan Brandy Company. Ararat is named for the biblical mountain where Noah landed; Noy is the Armenian version of Noah. Both companies claim to have launched the brandy industry in Armenia in 1877. Originally, a brandy distillery and ageing cellars were built on the site of a sixteenth-century Persian castle that commands a view of the approach to Yerevan. In 1899 this company was acquired by a Russian industrial magnate and brandy promoter named Nikolay Shustov, who is considered the father of the vital Armenian brandy industry. This industry played such a significant part in the country's history that a stamp with Shustov's picture was issued as recently as 2007.

Shustov's company became the official supplier to the royal court of Tsar Nicolas II in 1912. Throughout the Soviet era, these brandies were in great demand in Russia and other Soviet states. Stalin is said to have introduced Winston Churchill to Armenian brandy during the talks at Yalta in 1945. And Churchill apparently enjoyed it so much that it is said Stalin sent him a case every year for the rest of his life. (Another Churchill story follows, in the section on Georgian brandy.)

During the Soviet era the name of Shustov's company was changed to Yerevan, with production headquarters and

The Yerevan Brandy Company's Ararat brandies are presented with after-dinner sweets for a tasting in their modern conference room.

ageing cellars moved to a new, updated facility in the city in 1950. In 1998 the company was acquired by the international wine and spirits conglomerate Pernod Ricard and the company is now known as Ararat. Its modern production facility uses cognac-style distillation for its famous brandies. The Ararat company is now supplied by 5,000 grape growers and produces 5.5 million bottles a year, 92 per cent of which are exported to Russian and Baltic nations.

The Ararat cellars also hold a 'Peace Barrel', which melds 1994-vintage spirits from Armenia and Azerbaijan to represent the year of the ceasefire over the contested Nagorno-Karabakh region. The barrel was dedicated in 2001, and waits to be opened when there is a formal treaty of peace in the region.

After the demise of the Soviet Union, private investors scraped together enough money to start up production again at the original Shustov facility in 2002. They named their new venture Noy, and the company logo shows Noah's ark with the date 1877 on it. Apparently, the former company never moved all their original stores to the new location because today, deep underground, brandies that are close to 100 years old can be found in Noy's cellars. The Armenian brandy industry has come full circle: in 2011 Noy created a new line of brandy to supply the Kremlin.

Current labels at the historic Noy Brandy Company in Yerevan celebrate Noah landing on Armenia's Ararat Mountain. These bottles contain brandies aged for 10 and 20 years.

The Proshyan Brandy Company with its architectural ageing cellars
represents the modern international brandy industry in post-Soviet Armenia.

Proshyan, according to the owners of the company, is an
ancient, noble name; it is also the name of the village outside
Yerevan where this company is headquartered. There was a
'Proshyan Brandy Company' founded in 1887, but the current
company is not a direct descendant. It was not in existence in
the Soviet era, and though some of the company's production equipment dates from that time, it is now being augmented
by new machines from Italy. A new glass and marble office
building opened in 2012 to crown the old production yard.
A thoroughly modern corporation in feel, Proshyan produces
branded labels for 500 European supermarkets and sells to
Russia, Germany, the Baltic nations, South Korea and China.
Yet one of their claims to fame are their traditional, ornate
bottles in fascinating shapes from roses and ships to swords
and dragons. These 'souvenir' bottles account for a good 20
per cent of the market for Proshyan.

In direct contrast to this thriving enterprise is Vedi-Alco,
located at an old Soviet plant out in the countryside a couple

hours drive from Yerevan. It was taken over in 1996 by a group of workers desperate to improve their fortunes after the fall of the Soviet Union. The original factory was established in 1956, and the facilities still have a mid-twentieth-century Soviet feel. In 2000 the company started to distil brandy there again, and it also acquired some aged spirits. Currently the company does batch distillation in a column still, but hopes to be able to add a double-distilling system like the one it used to have – though repairing the roof has taken priority most recently. Demand is just starting to pick up, and Vedi-Alco brandy is now exported, mainly to the Russian market.

Culturally, brandy is considered a dessert beverage in Armenia. It can be served with chocolate, with oranges and apples, or with ripe, fresh peaches in season. Traditionally – as in many areas of the West – cigars also accompany brandy after dinner. Etiquette dictates that, when offered brandy in a snifter, a guest should be able to lay his glass down on its side and nothing will spill out; this signifies that the host has poured the correct amount for sipping, around 50 ml (about 1.7 fl. oz).

Currently, thirteen (mainly white) grapes can be used to make the wine for Armenian brandy: Azeteni, Banants, Chilar, Garan Dmak, Kakhet, Kangun, Lalvari, Masis, Meghrabujr, Mskhali, Rkatsiteli, Van and Voskehat.

During the Soviet era, the adjoining country of Georgia was known for its wine – though brandy has also been produced here since the late nineteenth century. For the past 130 years, Sarajishvili has been the most important Georgian brandy, founded by a Georgian native, David Sarajishvili, in 1884. After studying chemistry in Germany and distilling in Cognac, he had to return home after the death of his father. He sought out grapes that had similar characteristics to those used in Cognac from among the 500 varieties native to Georgia, selecting them from various regions of the country: Chinuri, Goruli

Created proudly in 1956, the Vedi-Alco company has struggled since
the Soviet Union's demise. Owned and managed by its workers, it now
produces wines and brandies with leftover Soviet-era equipment.
Armenia was the major brandy supplier to the Soviet Union in its heyday.

Sculptures adorn the grounds and steps of the Vedi-Alco company,
its grand entrance announced in Russian and Armenian.

Mtsvane, Kakhuri Mtsvane, Rkatsiteli, Tsitska and Tsolikouri. It has become customary for Georgian brandy producers to source grapes from around the country.

Sarajishvili also imported two additional significant elements from France: a copper alembic still from Cognac, and a connection to Camus Cognac, the area's oldest family-owned production company. This connection endured for decades but was severed during the Soviet era and then re-established afterwards, with the father of the current head of Camus.

An ancient Georgian drinking vessel with three connected cups was probably part of a drinking ceremony that originated thousands of years ago.

An embellished drinking horn carved from stone many millennia ago resides in the national museum in Tbilisi, Georgia.

Distilled from grape wine as in Cognac, Georgian Sarajishvili 'cognac' won medals and awards from the late 19th century on.

During the Soviet era the name of the firm was changed to the Tbilisi Brandy Company, and its products were often requisitioned by the authorities. Despite this, the distiller was somehow able to sequester a few historic barrels, including several made by David Sarajishvili himself in 1893 and 1905, which are in the cellars today. A little of the contents of these historic barrels is now blended into the company's top-of-the-line brandies.

Headquartered on a garden-like property established in Tbilisi in 1954, the Sarajishvili company was privatized in 1994 and continues to produce a range of aged brandies, double-distilled in its copper stills. Its chief technologist David Abzianidze carries the legacy of Sarajishvili brandy as a historian of the company and a forward-thinker for its products. However, he is not interested in having his brandies used in cocktails – as popular as this may be in other countries.

Abzianidze tells a (rather familiar) story learned from his predecessor: when Stalin gave Winston Churchill some Sarajishvili brandy during the Yalta talks in 1945, Churchill thought it was as fine as cognac, choosing it as the best brandy there.

Today several other Georgian companies are producing brandies, capitalizing on the status of Sarajishvili in particular and Georgian brandy in general. They may use grapes from any part of Georgia, and they bottle and market their products to countries familiar with Georgia's reputation. The wine company Tiflisi Marani is one – though it is better known for its wines at present. Another is KTW (Kakhetian Traditional Winemaking), a young company – literally – staffed by a group of fresh, energetic people. It was founded in 2001 and already has had great success in producing mid-priced wines and brandies for Eastern European and Baltic countries. KTW has

Though the brandies made here during the Soviet era may not have been of the same quality as before and after, the Sarajishvili company managed to retain its status as well as a spacious campus in Tbilisi with vine-covered buildings and a statue of the founder.

Sarajishvili 'cognac' was supplied to the royal family of Russia; this advertisement illustrates the power of the brand with rugged mountains and a conquering ram.

Created to appeal to traditionalists, the young company which named itself Kakhetian Traditional displays brandies and awards in its Tbilisi offices.

created a niche for itself with old-fashioned-style packaging, and many of their brandies have a homemade look in both bottle and flask shapes.

Though most of these Georgian and Armenian brandies have not yet reached the u.s. or uk markets, it is probably only a matter of time until more of them appear on the shelves – but perhaps they will reach the eager Asian market first.

6
Great Spanish and Latin Brandies

Though brandy is often considered to be a French drink, Spanish and Latin American cultures have strong brandy traditions that date back many centuries. In this chapter we take a look at brandies and their heritage on the Iberian Peninsula – and at the very important contribution of Peru.

Spain is the origin of a noble, Old World brandy that is not as well known as it should be today: brandy de Jerez. It is produced in the Jerez region, where sherry also originates. Jerez is in southwestern Spain, not far from the southern Atlantic coast near the Straits of Gibraltar. The sensory distinctiveness of brandy de Jerez comes not only from its geographic location but also from the unique ageing system for the brandies produced there. Brandy de Jerez and sherry are both aged with the same method, the *solera* system (discussed below). This practice imparts a unique flavour and aroma profile to the brandy: hints of marine salinity, vanilla and toasted caramel, carob and coffee notes, underlying layers reminiscent of mature oak and yeast.

Wine and other products have been traded in this part of Spain since the Phoenicians roamed its seas from around 700 to 500 BC. Wine was also exported during and after the time of the Roman Empire, until the Moorish occupation of the

Spain's brandy de Jerez is aged in oak barrels, gaining colour from the oak and evolving from a clear liquid through hues of yellow, gold, amber and mahogany-brown.

Iberian Peninsula from AD 711 to 1492. Though the Moors traditionally did not drink wine in accordance with Islamic laws, they made use of the grapes in the existing vineyards to produce an alcohol distillate for use in medicines, cosmetics and perfumes.

When the Moors were driven back towards the south – and eventually out of Iberia – their distilling technology remained. Local medical and alchemical specialists employed the process to create their own 'waters of life' and 'waters of the spirit'. In fact, *aguardiente* (from *aqua ardens*, the 'burning water' of the Middle Ages) is still the generic Spanish term for brandy.

Though the first reference to brandy in Jerez appears in 1580 in relation to a tax on spirits, brandy could have been

manufactured there earlier. In this Spanish region, as in France, it was the Dutch who exploited the manufacture of brandy beginning in the late sixteenth century. Today the clear spirit that comes off the pot stills to be aged into brandy is still called *holandas*. And many streets, pavements and patios in Jerez de la Frontera are lined with the small, rounded stones brought from Holland centuries ago as ballast for ships that took on cargoes of distilled spirits in Jerez.

Through the eighteenth century, this Spanish brandy was shipped unaged; in fact, under the *gremio* (grape growers' league) law, *holandas* was required to be shipped out every year so the growers and distillers could empty their cellars before the next harvest, and get paid for their products promptly.

Legend has it that in the early nineteenth century, a shipment of *aguardiente* was put into used sherry casks, ready to be shipped out. But the ship left without these casks, which were

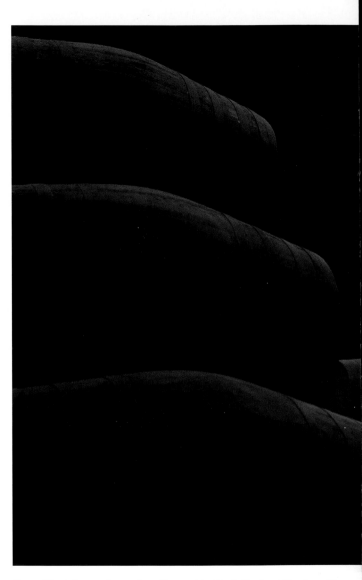

One of Spain's most famous brandies, world-wide, is Cardenal Mendoza. Here it is ageing in casks at Sanchez Romate in Jerez, Spain, before being bottled.

only discovered later. After tasting this spirit, the producers realized that it had improved in the barrels, and this is how barrel-ageing brandy de Jerez began. The producer was the famous company now known as Pedro Domecq, and the year was 1818.

Production and trade of brandy from the Jerez area increased steadily through the nineteenth century. The brandy was originally made with the region's native Palomino grape (also used in sherry), but with the brandy boom in the late nineteenth century, producers had to look farther afield. They found the required characteristics in Airén grapes, grown in the centre of Spain in the Castilla-La Mancha region.

A large proportion of the grapes for brandy de Jerez is still grown in Castilla-La Mancha. Wine from these grapes is made in the La Mancha city of Tomelloso, where many brandy producers also own distilleries. However, brandy blending and ageing is always done in the Jerez area, specifically in the designated coastal 'sherry triangle' area bounded by the towns of Jerez, El Puerto de Santa Maria and Sanlúcar de Barrameda. Some brandy is also distilled in Jerez.

For brandy de Jerez, both pot stills and column stills are used. Technically, when a still is heated by steam it is called an alembic, and when it is heated by wood it is an *alquitara*. The spirits from both types of stills are classified as *holandas de vino*.

The Jerez barrel-ageing warehouses (bodegas) and their offices are generally whitewashed adobe structures a few storeys high, with orange-red terracotta roof tiles. Many are set up like miniature versions of a nineteenth-century villa located in the heart of the city of Jerez: warrens of buildings behind walls, all charmingly accented with deep-red bougainvillea. Airy and pleasant year-round, each hive of business contains white buildings connected by brown cobbled lanes, often interspersed with gardens or open squares.

A typical bodega for ageing in Jerez, Spain.

Brandy de Jerez barrels (previously used for sherry) are made of American oak, a custom that began when the region first became a prosperous Atlantic trading zone. Barrels that have been used to age different styles of sherry – from sweet to dry – are selected to shape the aromas and flavours of the brandies.

Brandy de Jerez is produced solely by the *solera* method, which according to legend was due to another fortunate accident. In 1870, numerous barrels of brandy were left unclaimed in the corner of a bodega. Someone discovered the barrels in 1874, but they could not sell the entire quantity of such old brandy right away, so they began mixing it, filtering down some newer brandy into the barrels to fill the space left by normal evaporation. This was so successful in contributing complexity and finesse to the aged spirit that the *solera* method has been used ever since.

In the *solera* method, barrels of brandy are stacked according to age in the high-ceilinged bodegas. The top row of casks contains the youngest brandies, and each successive row of casks contains increasingly older brandies down to the floor level (*solera* level). When some of the matured brandy is removed from the floor-level casks for bottling, the floor-level casks are topped up from the next row above, and those from the row above of them, and so on. The rows above the *solera* are called *criaderas* – a charming word meaning 'nurseries'. Commonly, there are at least three or four vertical rows of casks ageing in the bodegas, with plenty of air space above.

During the dry heat of summer, the red-brown clay floors of the bodegas are sprinkled with water to maintain humidity and limit evaporation from the barrels. Since the percentage of brandy evaporation from barrels can reach up to 7 per cent per year, at some bodegas systems for temperature and humidity control are starting to be introduced. Though these may help a company's bottom line, it remains to be seen whether the brandies will retain their unique, regional aromas and flavours without the natural breezes blowing through the bodegas.

In Jerez, the top sherry producers also tend to produce the top-quality brandies. However, they do not make the best-selling brandy. That distinction belongs to Bodegas Terry with its Centenario brandy. Terry was founded by an Irish family in the mid-nineteenth century. They named their brandy 'Centenario' when they established new facilities in the near-by town of Santa Maria at the beginning of the century – the twentieth century, that is.

Another of the most famous brandies from Jerez is the ubiquitous Cardenal Mendoza, produced by Sánchez Romate since 1887. Originally made for the owners' private consumption, it was soon commercialized and is now known around the world.

Some bodegas buy spirit to age, while others have the facilities to do more of their own distilling, such as the 150-year-old

González Byass and the eighteenth-century Pedro Domecq (now part of Bodegas Fundador). Occasionally, a newer company appears, like Bodegas Tradición (established in 1998), which has been buying stores of brandies from a variety of sources to further age, blend and bottle under its own label.

Though brandy has been made in Jerez for centuries, the Consejo Regulador (Regulatory Council) for brandy de Jerez was established only in 1987. According to the Council, three styles of brandy de Jerez may be defined, by their increasing amounts of 'volatile components' and also by the classification of age: brandy de Jerez Solera, aged for an average of a year and a half; brandy de Jerez Solera Reserva, which is aged for three years on average; and brandy de Jerez Solera Gran Reserva, which averages ten years of age.

Small amounts of brandy have also been made in other areas of Spain since the boom in the late 1800s. In the northeastern region of Catalonia, brandy was historically one source of the calories people in this mountainous terrain needed to survive in the harsh climate. As late as the end of the twentieth century – and possibly still today – a custom existed whereby workmen would stop in a café in the morning on the way to their jobs to have a coffee topped up with brandy, for energy.

An example of a Catalonian brandy producer is Mascaró, a company founded at the end of the Second World War. Historically, many Catalonians became rum distillers in the Spanish colonies, and exported their products back to Spain. But during the Spanish Civil War and in subsequent disruptions of trade through the Second World War, Spain stopped importing spirits. So Catalonians had to start distilling their own spirits at home with the materials on hand, namely wine.

Located near the French border, Catalonians such as Narciso Mascaró (the son of a wine merchant and distiller) chose to use the Charentais or Cognac method of double distilling. The Spanish sparkling wine cava is also made in this area, and cava grapes lend themselves readily to distilling. The Parellada grape, which has high acidity and delicate aromas, is the basis for many Catalonian brandies; Macabeu and Xarel·lo are also used.

Portugal, also part of the Iberian Peninsula, produces some brandy too, notably in Lourinhã. This historic area of brandy production received DOC (Denominaçao de Origem Controlada, or PDO, Protected Designation of Origin) status only twenty years ago, though there has been a tradition of brandy distilling there since the eighteenth century. Lourinhã is located in a wine-making region north of Lisbon and the brandy made there is referred to by the traditional Portuguese term, *aguardente*.

Across the Atlantic, one of Spain's former colonies, Mexico, has followed the lead of its erstwhile mother country in brandy production. Mexican brandies are also made by the *solera* method, though in general they have not been considered as fine as Spain's brandies. Until the twenty-first century, almost all of Mexico's wine grapes were used for brandy distillation. Its most famous brandy is Presidente, which is produced in Mexico by Pedro Domecq of Jerez and also exported to many countries around the world.

Until the beginning of the nineteenth century the Philippines were governed by a colonial administration headquartered not in Spain but in Mexico, and Mexico has therefore been an influence on Filipino culture. Both Spanish and Mexican brandies have made their way to the Philippines, where Spain's Fundador is also a very important brandy. Local brands Emperador and Generoso are the other top sellers there.

Meanwhile, back in the sixteenth century, there was a parallel development of brandy going on in South America, especially in Peru, home of the brandy called pisco. Though many people do not realize it, pisco is a brandy. Pisco differs from other brandies in that it is a white (clear) spirit, and no water is added after distilling. In other words, the spirit must come off the still with the desired level of alcohol for bottling, which is between 38 and 43 per cent. Brandy de Jerez, cognac and most other brandies are distilled to a higher alcohol level before water is gradually blended in during the months before bottling.

Pisco originated as early as the beginning of the seventeenth century along the southern coast of the country, where grapes had been grown since the mid-sixteenth century. It is named after the port city of Pisco, the shipping point for much of this brandy. Spanish explorers and settlers had brought grapes from the Canary Islands and from Spain to plant near Peru's south coast because wine was part of their religion and culture.

Fundador brandy was created over 100 years ago, when it was sold in bottles like this, wrapped in papers marked with the full name of the town where the brandy is aged: Jerez de la Frontera, Spain.

This area proved so prolific for grapes that in a short time wine was being exported from Peru to Spain. But Spanish wine-makers strongly protested against competition from colonial imports so a law was enacted in 1641 banning the importation of Peruvian wine. So Peruvian winemakers began distilling their wine into brandy (*aguardiente de vino*) and exporting that to Spain, where it found a ready market.

Originally, Peruvian brandy could be distilled in either of two types of stills. The *falca* looked like one of the early Moorish or medieval stills: a simple container for heating and a long pipe for condensing the vapours. Peru's other type of still, its alembic, was more sophisticated, like the European alembic stills with their long, spiral necks of copper tubing. In this latter process heads and tails were discarded and the pure heart of the pisco vapour remained, to be cooled and poured into clay *botijas* for shipping.

Though pisco was imported into the San Francisco area during the seventeenth and eighteenth centuries, a demand for pisco intensified when the Gold Rush pioneers arrived in California in the mid-nineteenth century. Pisco's renown only increased during the course of the rest of the century. In the early 1900s, San Francisco was the seat of a pisco craze: people couldn't get enough of it. Often they drank it in a Pisco Punch, said to have been invented in San Francisco. Pisco Punch, a concoction with lemon, sugar and pineapple, also spread across California to Nevada, according to newspaper articles of the time.

As wildly popular as pisco and Pisco Punch were in the West in the early part of the twentieth century, Prohibition effectively destroyed the pisco market in the u.s. Afterwards, pisco declined into a notoriously rough, cheap spirit – the type of drink one would expect at a bar in an old western movie set in California.

But pisco was not dead; in fact, at the turn of the millennium it was ready for resurrection. Authentic pisco was being rediscovered by travellers to Peru, and producers again began to have a market for a finer version of pisco. Though pisco had been made for centuries, it was only in 1999 that Peruvian producers created their own Denomination of Origin rules for the area of production, the types and quality of grapes, and the distillation and ageing of the spirit.

Barely a decade into the twenty-first century, pisco began a new upswing in popularity, especially within the current mixology movement. Today the spirit is produced as pisco puro (from a single grape variety) or as pisco acholado, from more than one grape, and usually with grapes that are both aromatic and non-aromatic.

Pisco can also be made either from wine that is fully fermented, or from wine that is partially fermented (still somewhat sweet); and sometimes it is made from a mixture of the two. Pisco can be made from eight grapes: the aromatic grape varieties blended into pisco are Italia, Torontel, Moscatel, and Albilla, while non-aromatic piscos (which are more typical) tend to be made from the grapes Quebranta, Mollar, Negra Criolla, and Uvina. Quebranta is by far the dominant grape in Peru's pisco.

As much as Peru has been identified with pisco for centuries, today it is not the only country that makes this spirit: Chile has launched an effort to compete on the world pisco market. Historically, a pisco-style brandy had been made in Chile, though even as recently as a decade ago in Chile it was common to look to Peru for the better piscos. But not any more.

Chilean piscos, however, are quite different from Peru's in aromas and flavours – Chile's tend to be softer and more fragrant. Currently, several producers in Chile are making very good piscos in cognac-style double-distillation stills with aromatic Muscat grapes, notably companies like Kappa (from the winemaking Marnier-Lapostolle family) and ABA. They are using high-quality wine grapes, and it shows in the final product.

Though the pisco industry is still dominated by Peru, Chile actually has had its own pisco denomination since 1936, when a town in the grape-growing region of Elqui changed its name to 'Pisco Elqui'. And Chilean producers are also experimenting with another cognac element: barrel-ageing.

Fine brandy-making is found somewhat randomly in the rest of Latin America. In Argentina, for instance, Ramefort Coñac was started with advice from cognac producers, and its brandies are made in the cognac style. On the other hand, Bolivia has its own special style of brandy called *singani*; distilled mainly from high-altitude-grown Muscat grapes, it is a unique spirit.

After this exhaustive tour of Spanish-inspired brandies, it is a toss-up whether one would want to relax with a sipping-glass of brandy de Jerez, or a Pisco Sour cocktail – before we continue on our world tour of brandy.

7
Australia and South Africa

Whether they brought the taste for it from their home country or developed it abroad, inhabitants of the British Empire were robust consumers of brandy. And, as mentioned earlier, brandy was also regarded as a household staple for medicinal purposes – a state of affairs that lasted well into the twentieth century.

Located far from Europe, British Commonwealth countries, most notably South Africa and Australia, made their own brandies for domestic consumption. In Australia, Château Tanunda is an example of a well-established brand that has been recognized for more than a century. This brandy comes from one of the first areas in the country where grapes were planted, the Barossa Valley in South Australia. Château Tanunda was established there some decades later, in 1890, but the grandeur of its estate and the company's savvy salesmanship ensured that Tanunda's brandy became known as 'the Commonwealth's hospital brandy'.

Brandy was firmly believed to be a cure for all types of problems. In fact, brandy is credited for a sports career, when in 1896 the famed cricket batsman Frank Iredale was 'Saved from Failure by Brandy and Soda', as a *Perth Daily News* headline declared.

Australia's Château Tanunda has made wines and brandies since the late 1800s, and today the Château Tanunda brandies are an still extremely popular brand.

The grapes planted in the Barossa Valley in Australia in the mid-nineteenth century were used for both wine and brandy. Syrupy-sweet fortified wines, sherry-style wines and heavy brandies were very popular in Australia from the mid-1800s. Unfortunately, it seems the Australian perception of brandy has been trapped in the past – few younger people today are interested in brandy. Brandy is considered an acceptable spirit, but in a curiously limited way: it is consumed mainly by women over the age of 40, say Australian brandy producers.

Though the Angove family had been making wine since 1855 in Australia, they started growing grapes specifically for brandy in 1910. Carl Angove opened the first industrial distillery there in 1925. He followed the French and Spanish model, using grapes that were fairly neutral but could be harvested with good acidity: the table grape Sultana, as well as the French Colombard and Spanish Palomino. Angove brandy was a bit of a departure from the heavy, sweet style most Australians had been used to in wines as well as in spirits. It was considered more of a clean, cognac-style brandy, and it was very well received – as it is today. Angove's St Agnes brand has over 70 per cent of the market in its native state of South Australia, and 40 per cent of the country's brandy market. And Angove is reportedly the only company still making their brandies in a Charente-style pot still, double-distilled.

In addition to Angove and Château Tanunda, the most popular brandies in the country are Hardy's Black Bottle brand and the Woolworths-distributed brand from France called Napoleon 1875; French cognac by Rémy Martin also does well there. Brandy consumption in Australia has been extremely stable for some time. And there has been no traction in the movement for brandy cocktails. But very recently there has been a new development: China. Enamoured with European brandies, the Chinese are also looking at other sources to supply their high-end brandy appetite. Suddenly, they have become interested in, for instance, Angove's xo, and this may be the beginning of a new trend.

In contrast to Australia, in India the major brandy consumers are men. The high-end spirits they drink are usually imported from Cognac. But at the middle to lower range, the spirits are likely to have been manufactured in India. Lacking a significant amount of native grapes and grape wine, manufacturers in India often distil their spirits out of sugar products – so technically these spirits would all be rums, not brandies or whiskies. But they are coloured, sometimes aged and/or flavoured, labelled as brandy or whisky and sold to a public that has become used to this style of spirit. So-called 'brandies' that are manufactured in other high brandy consumption countries in Asia (such as Malaysia and the Philippines) are also more than likely to be produced by the same rum-like process domestically.

In contrast, another former Commonwealth country, South Africa, has a strong cognac-style brandy orientation

Angove Family Winemakers began producing their well-known St Agnes brandy in Australia in 1925.

due to its roots as a Dutch colony dating back to 1652. Early settlers had planted grapes in South Africa by 1659. The popular account of brandy's beginnings in South Africa mentions a Dutch ship named *De Pijl*, which first distilled brandy there while it was anchored offshore on 19 May 1672. As mentioned earlier, the Dutch were responsible for distilling wine into brandy in several areas of France in the seventeenth century, so they had the knowledge and equipment to do this wherever they found suitable grapes.

With plenty of white grapes to distil, South Africa's brandy industry grew in parallel to its wine industry. Brandy is made here mainly from Chenin Blanc and Colombard (which in South Africa is often spelled Colombar, without the final 'd').

For several centuries, virtually all of South Africa's brandies were designated for domestic consumption. One notable early brandy enterprise was Van Ryn, established in 1845. After buying out F. C. Collison (which was established in 1833) it has laid claim to being the oldest continuous brandy making concern in the country. Van Ryn distils brandies in a cognac style, and even has its own on-site cooperage.

South Africa's largest brandy producer is KWV (Koöperatieve Wijnbouwers Vereniging van Zuid-Afrika), a company that was founded in 1918; it became a winemaking cooperative in 1923 and began brandy production in 1926. During its history, this cooperative has been both a private and a public company at various times. As the regulator of the South African wine industry until 1977, KWV exported its bottled brandies because it was not allowed to compete on the domestic market – though it did sell brandy in bulk to other companies which then aged and bottled it. Currently, it is a private company that both exports and sells domestically – and remains very important in the South African brandy and wine market.

Evolving with the times, St Agnes has updated bottles and labels to indicate its quality on the world market.

In South Africa, brandy production has always proceeded along traditional lines, as seen in this copper alembic still at Van Ryn.

Another significant company, Klipdrift, started out in 1938 as a small, backyard distillery but rose in record time to become South Africa's best-known brandy. Unfortunately, this is one of the brandies that fuelled the decline of South African brandy in both quality and perception. By the middle of the twentieth century, much South African domestic brandy had become the equivalent of cheap rum in America. 'Klippies and cola', like rum and Coke in the u.s., represented a basic, low-end drink. And then there was '1-2-3' (also sometimes called '3-2-1'), the downscale version of a fun evening: 1 litre of brandy, 2 litres of cola and a 3-litre Ford.

But in the last few years, changes have begun to be felt in the industry. Just as rum brands in the u.s. have worked very hard to upgrade their image from rum-and-Coke status, South Africans have begun to prove their spirits are worthy of a better standing in the spirits industry and have introduced quite a few fine, aged brandies to both their domestic and export markets.

The South African Brandy Foundation was founded in 1984. It has standardized brandy production into four categories. The first level is called Blended Brandy and is made to be used in mixed drinks; it requires a minimum of 30 per cent pot-still brandy aged in oak for at least three years, and the remainder can be neutral, unaged spirit. The second level, Vintage Brandy, requires at least 30 per cent pot-still brandy with up to 60 per cent column-still spirit matured for at least eight years, and up to 10 per cent wine spirits (unmatured). The third level, Potstill Brandy, must have a minimum of 90 per cent pot-still brandy and a maximum of 10 per cent neutral unaged spirit. The fourth category, Estate Brandy, must be entirely produced, aged and bottled on one estate; it is always labelled with the word 'estate' as well as the type of brandy.

Label terms like vs and vsop may be used, but they do not have the same ageing designation as in Cognac. South African brandies must be aged in 340-litre French oak casks for a minimum of three years. *Solera* ageing is also allowed in South Africa. Though there is not a designated brandy production area, grapes for the South African brandies tend to come from major wine-grape growing areas including Worcester, Olifants River, Orange River, Breede River and Klein Karoo.

Brandy continues to be the top-selling spirit in South Africa. In 2008 a new annual festival called Fine Brandy Fusion was launched, mainly to attract attention from younger consumers and to position brandy as high-end and glamorous. Interestingly, today the South African Brandy Foundation website also harks back to the origins of distilled spirits with this lyrical description: 'Making brandy is akin to alchemy, when nature's elements – earth, wind, water and fire – are transformed into gold.'

8
Brandy Made in America

Historically, brandy was considered a household necessity in the United States, for uses ranging from drinks to medical remedies; in fact brandy was classified as a medicine until the early twentieth century. In the eastern u.s., cognac and other French brandies were imported. But in the west of the country there was little commercially available brandy, except for Peruvian pisco.

After the population explosion in the west in the late nineteenth century, there was a new hunger for brandies there. Two of the legacy brandy companies in the United States began their production in the 1880s: Christian Brothers in 1882 and Korbel in 1889. Francis Korbel was a Bohemian immigrant who, with his brothers, was drawn to California's unlimited opportunities after the Gold Rush. He found land north of San Francisco, where he began making sparkling wine. After mastering wine production and marketing, Korbel went on to do the same with brandy.

Korbel may – or may not – have been influenced by the success of a lay religious order that had begun crafting and selling brandy a few years earlier, to finance their educational mission. Production and distillation by Christian Brothers (and many later entrants into California's commercial brandy business) were headquartered in the state's fertile inland valley, where a large percentage of California's fruits and vegetables were grown. Here, start-up brandy producers had access to quantities of inexpensive grapes and many of them began production with common table grapes like Thompson's Seedless and Flame Tokay. Later, more wine grapes were raised in this region, some of which were also used in brandy production.

Brandy producers typically tried to copy cognac's selection of raw material: producers believed they had to use grapes that did not have the potential to make great wines in order to produce wonderful brandies. That was true to an extent, especially if the grapes had aromatic components like florals that could transcend the distillation process. And these types of grapes could be picked earlier, with higher acidity and lower sugars, so they could be bought more cheaply: less time on the vine meant less time and expense caring for the vineyards before harvest each season.

Several decades after commercial brandy production began in California, Prohibition put a stop to winemaking. Because of its supposed medicinal qualities, cognac was the only liquor allowed to be imported into the u.s. during Prohibition. Brandy had ceased to be classed a medicine in the u.s. a few years before Prohibition, but many doctors continued to prescribe it and brandy was considered as much a part of a household medicine kit as Band-Aids are today. There are no comprehensive records of brandy being produced in the u.s. during Prohibition, but home brandy-making kits were available then – though people used whatever fruits they had available for fermentation.

Just as Prohibition nearly killed the consumer wine industry in California, it also left brandy production in need of its own restorative after Repeal. A number of individuals from across California stepped into the breach and began distilling and distributing commercial brandies again. These producers included Giovanni Vai in the Cucamonga Valley (1933), Antonio Perelli-Minetti in Delano (1936), George Zaninovich in Fresno (1937), and two brothers, Ernest and Julio Gallo (1939). Apparently, the E. & J. Gallo company got into the brandy business because there were a few bumper crops of wine grapes in the years right after Repeal. When there is more wine than can be sold, it is common to distil the wine into spirits for a variety of uses. Brandy, as an unaged spirit, was also used to fortify the sweet wines that were very popular in the u.s. for most of the twentieth century.

At the beginning, Ernest Gallo bought a few thousand barrels of brandy from a friend, to help him out. Then, in 1949, the Gallo company decided to use its 'surplus' wine to produce Gallo brandy. They produced a new product, Eden Roc brandy, in 1967. The company released Gallo brandy again in 1973, when they opened their own distillery in Fresno. Eden Roc was discontinued in 1975, when the expensive-looking E&J brandy was introduced. The company used the traditional Cognac grape Colombard, along with some Chenin Blanc, Grenache, Barbera and Moscato. E&J brandy was first distributed nationally in 1977; at that time Julio Gallo began producing his own single-variety brandies as well.

Christian Brothers and Korbel started producing brandy again after Prohibition. Additional large corporations also began making brandies to fill an increasing demand in the u.s. Many of these companies were also the producers of the most popular mid-century American wine brands such as Almaden, Italian Swiss Colony and Paul Masson. In the mid-1950s more than a dozen producers in California were making fashionable lines of grape-wine-based brandies. Large u.s. distributors also stepped in to fund and/or partner with the producers in this profitable industry; the four largest

To differentiate themselves from other brandies of lesser quality, California wine pioneers Ernest and Julio Gallo created a label that read simply 'E&J' for their brandies in the early 20th century.

distributors were Seagram's, Schenley, National Distillers and Hiram Walker & Sons.

California brandy was in such demand for the next few decades that the biggest companies found it expedient, after distilling, to transport the brandy to Kentucky, where there were giant sheds full of used bourbon barrels that could be used to age the brandies. Though they advertised their ageing, producers generally omitted to mention where their 'California brandy' was aged.

With increased production came decreases in production quality. Though many companies started out hand-crafting brandies in cognac-style pot stills for part or all of their distilling, most moved to industrial, high-volume column stills (nothing like the small, artisanal column stills in Armagnac). They had to keep up with a demand that was not very quality-conscious at this time. After the middle of the twentieth century a confluence of factors nearly sounded a death knell for the reputation of California brandies: lesser-quality domestic production, a generation of young people who rejected their parents' drinks, and an increase in people of all ages who travelled and experienced fine brandies in other countries.

But there remained – and still remains – a faction of U.S. consumers favouring stalwart U.S. brands like Christian Brothers, E. & J. Gallo, Korbel and Paul Masson. With their Kentucky associations, two of the 'big four' U.S. brandy producers were eventually acquired by conglomerates that had originated as

California wine producers Korbel stuck to a traditional, almost medicinal look for their early brandies – after all, brandy has been considered medicinal for centuries.

This photograph shows an early Korbel calling card. Taken near the turn of the century, we can see the winery employees posing for this group shot in front of the old Brandy Tower. It's interesting to note that the Brandy Tower does not have the steel reinforcing rings which were added after the San Francisco earthquake and fire of 1906.

This photo of the Korbel production facility in Northern California shows it well-established in San Francisco before 1906.

producers and/or distributors of bourbon: Christian Brothers by (the appropriately named) Heaven Hill and Paul Masson by Constellation Brands. But with many of these brandies sold at low-end prices, the industry's status also declined – deservedly or not. California brandies had fallen out of favour with the young and the elite by the 1980s.

This is where the situation stood for several decades, until the comparatively recent rise in cognac's popularity. Some of the long-established u.s. brandies have risen with the tide, and all have begun to repackage and reposition their brands. For example, Gallo started producing an alembic brandy in 2003. With 43 per cent of the market, the company

Korbel brandy is presented here as a fine drink for upmarket society; this advertisement shows a popular fighter admired by discerning gentlemen and ladies.

KORBEL BRANDY

A SPLENDID LEGACY
of San Francisco's Golden Age

Pompadour Jim recounts the felling of "The Boston Strong Boy."

Fresh from his triumph over John L. Sullivan, Pompadour Jim Corbett light-heartedly revealed the training regimen that enabled him to go 21 rounds and win the brawl of the Century.

When asked if he trained with a "Barbary Breakfast"...brandy with a beer chaser...our former bank clerk and now World Champion simply smiled.

There was a time, a golden city and Korbel.

KORBEL OF CALIFORNIA

KORBEL BRANDY

HEIR TO THE RICH TRADITION OF THE KORBEL CHAMPAGNE CELLARS

is currently riding the crest of a few recent trends: an increase in younger consumers, and an increase in women opting for brandy.

As will be discussed, a more positive perception of u.s. brandy may be influenced by the release of new high-end products, by an awareness of brandy that has overflowed from the burgeoning artisan spirits movement, and by a new appreciation of cognac and brandy developed within this century's mixology craze.

9
Everything You Need to Know about Cognac

When we last immersed ourselves in Cognac, it was early in the twentieth century and the region was recovering nicely from the European grapevine plague that had decimated its vineyards. At the same time, cognac was threatened by brandy producers who had sprung up in other countries during the late nineteenth century – and who were also calling their spirits 'cognac'.

In order to characterize the uniqueness of their brandy, the people of Cognac first sought to create a delimited area for cognac vineyards. Then they codified the production and ageing requirements for their spirits. Later, they went after trade agreements with other brandy-producing regions, attempting to restrict the use of the word 'cognac' – a crusade that continues today.

Based on the most comprehensive land analysis of the region (from 1860), the first version of the delimited area was completed in 1909. Cognac became an AOC (Appellation d'Origine Contrôlée, controlled designation of origin) region in 1936, and Cognac's borders were finalized in 1938 with six growing areas (*crus*): Grande Champagne, Petite Champagne, Borderies, Fins Bois, Bons Bois, and Bois à Terroirs (also known as Bois Ordinaires). Fine Champagne is an additional appellation but not a growing area; it refers to a cognac blended from Grande and Petite Champagne grapes, with at least 50 per cent from Grande Champagne.

'Champagne' here means 'countryside' and it is a chalky soil whose vineyards provide the grapes that make the best cognacs. Grande Champagne vineyards are considered the top of the line, with Petite Champagne (a different type of chalk) a close second. After these, hierarchically, run Borderies (with more clay and sand), Fins Bois and Bons Bois (with varying amounts and types of chalk in their soil), then Bois Ordinaires (with more sand).

It used to be that only the top two or three *crus* were made into the top-priced cognacs, but now producers are experimenting successfully with finely aged cognacs blended from the other *crus* as well. Recently, Camus came out with a line of Île de Ré cognacs which have salty, peaty, whisky-like smoky aromas and flavours. It is particularly fitting that this line of cognacs may expose more people to cognac, because the superior salt harvested on the Île de Ré was a factor in early Dutch trading leading to the creation of the spirit of cognac itself.

Only white grape varieties may be used to make cognac. The main grapes in Cognac are Colombard, Folle Blanche and Ugni Blanc. In addition, cognac producers may use up to 10 per cent of Folignan, Jurançon Blanc, Meslier Saint-François, Montils, Sélect, and Sémillon (each representing a maximum of 10 per cent). Cognac producers are already thinking about which grapes will do best in upcoming years if climate change progresses quickly.

Cognac must be produced with double distillation, and it must be aged in the fine oak barrels coopered in the region, with wood from nearby forests. Local Limousin oak, with its looser wood grain, is considered best for extracting the most desirable characteristics for brandy. The trees are carefully chosen, then the wood is cut, split and air dried for two to three years.

These costly barrels are constructed by hand. Each cognac producer may decide how the inside of the barrels will be toasted: some prefer it lighter and some darker, depending on the sensory features they want to impart to their spirits. (Though cognac ideally gains most of its colour from ageing in barrels, legally, some caramel colouring may be added, as well as sugar and a wood 'tea' called *boisé* for the final blending.) When cognac ages naturally, it moves from clear through yellow then tan into golden amber and tawny colours, and at ten years old it will be a rich, mahogany brown.

Through it all, producers must take into account evaporation, which ranges from 2 to 6 per cent per year. This evaporated amount is called the 'angels' share'. In French it's *la part des anges*, which is also the name of Cognac's annual charity auction, one which attracts high-end international bidders.

This photograph shows the development of the colour of cognac as it ages, from clear through straw-gold, amber and brown, over the course of two and a half decades.

Cognacs are aged in both dry and humid cellars, some-times being moved every year or so (typically just the contents, not the barrels) in a complicated scheme developed to maxi-mize desirable aromas and flavours. In humid cellars the alcohol evaporates faster and the cognacs become rounder, softer, with more fruit and floral characteristics. Dry cellars have relatively faster water evaporation, and these conditions contribute more spicy and woody notes to the cognacs.

Distillers and cellar masters each have their own individ-ual formulas for generating the particular taste profiles of their cognacs. These sensory elements range from floral through citrus, to baking spices and cigar-box-like aromas, and include innumerable other components like toffee, coffee, cedar, leather, dried fruits and vanilla.

Even after cognac's production methods were standard-ized, the rest wasn't quite smooth sailing. During the Second World War much of the area was occupied, but the far-sighted cognac producers were able to preserve much of their stocks for the future. Just how this was accomplished is not a story that is commonly told to visitors because it is said that some of the producers may have made deals with the devil; for those interested in the specifics there are more details in lengthier books on cognac's history.

The Cognac Bureau (the BNIC or Bureau National Inter-professionnel du Cognac) was created after the Second World War, in 1946, to monitor cognac's production and distribu-tion both at home and throughout the world. Its plenary board consists of seventeen grape growers and seventeen cognac houses. According to BNIC rules, grapes for cognac must be made into a wine that is not aged; the wine must be distilled into an *eau de vie* as soon as possible. In Cognac, the distillations must be finished by 1 April of the year after the harvest. A cognac officially cannot be sold to the public until it has been barrel-aged for at least two years after the 1 April distillation limit.

One well-known cognac house, Hine, prides itself on continuing the practice of making a style of cognac that was very common until the mid-twentieth century. Called 'early landed' cognac, it is shipped to Britain in barrels and aged in a warehouse there before bottling. In England's year-round cool and damp climate, less evaporation occurs and the flavour profile is somewhat different from Cognac-aged spirits. (Hine has also been the official cognac supplier to Queen Elizabeth II for the past 50 years.)

It is important to note that all of the development of a cognac occurs during its barrel-ageing: once bottled, the cognac is ready to drink. It does not further improve in the bottle. Even in the barrel, at some point a cognac ceases to develop. This takes decades, up to as much as 80 years. At that point, if the cognac is not being bottled for sale, the cellar master will transfer it to a large, rounded glass container called a *dame-jeanne* (demijohn) and place it reverently in the gated and locked room that guards the producer's most precious cognacs. This area of the cellar is called, appropriately, the *paradis* (paradise).

Once opened, a bottle of cognac will keep for months or even up to a year in a cool, dark location. The best phase for drinking a cognac may be only a few years after bottling for a lesser-aged cognac, while it can stretch to decades for an older one. Though eventually even a bottled cognac's flavours and aromas will begin to fade.

Requirements for current cognac styles were finalized in 1983; and though future changes are being discussed, they are not guaranteed. Currently, these are the categories listed on the Cognac Bureau's website: VS (Very Special) or 3-star is *compte 2*, with at least two years of barrel age; VSOP (Very Superior Old Pale) or Reserve means *compte 4*, or at least four years of barrel ageing; Napoléon, xo (Extra Old) or Hors d'âge indicates *compte 6*, or at least six years of barrel-ageing. The category of the cognac reflects the age of the youngest brandy in the blend. Vintage-category cognacs, which have recently become popular, must contain spirits distilled from only one designated harvest. Most of the cognac sold (about 85 per cent) is vs or vsop, with the rest being older cognacs.

There has been some confusion about the term Napoléon because it has been used indiscriminately in the past by producers in Cognac (and in the rest of the world) to imply that a brandy is very old. In Cognac, the term Napoléon now officially means the cognac has been aged at least six years, the same as an xo cognac. To further complicate things, in practice a cognac labelled with the word 'Extra' is often older than an xo. Many xo and Extra cognacs have a significant percentage of much older cognacs blended in; the exact components in the blend are different at each cognac house. Lately, cognac houses have also been releasing speciality cognacs with proprietary names and distinctive labels to capture the attention of different types of consumers.

Designations like vs, vsop and xo have been co-opted by many countries, even those that no longer use the term 'cognac'. This labelling is convenient because it can – if employed honestly – tell buyers whether to expect a more- or less-aged product, within that particular system. However, each brandy-producing region has its own rules for ageing and labelling, so a vsop from another region may not be the same age (or made with the same care) as a vsop from Cognac.

At present, the Cognac Bureau lists 325 cognac producers, including small and large companies, individuals and cooperatives. But four major companies eclipse most of the others in that their names are practically household words worldwide: Courvoisier, Hennessy, Martel and Rémy Martin. They are

Each cognac producer may keep decades of samples of aged cognacs on hand, both for reference and to create a perfect blend for special occasions.

responsible for about 85 per cent of Cognac's production. These companies own some vineyards, they distil some cognac from wine supplied by grape growers, and they also subscribe to the common practice of buying distilled spirit from growers and then ageing, blending, bottling and marketing the cognac.

Bottles these days range from cylindrical to flask-shaped, but there are many other curvy, seductive glass forms and contours. Producers commission amazing, sculptural shapes for their top cognacs; at this level the bottle itself adds significantly to the value of the cognac. Labels also vary widely in motif. They can appear ancient and traditional or be so completely postmodern that there are barely two words on the front of the bottle. All in all, design can add so tremendously to the prestige and price of a cognac that a few top-of-the-line bottles sell for thousands of dollars – or even tens of thousands. Single bottles of Hennessy, Hine and Courvoisier, for example, have sold for U.S. $10,000 (£6,000) in the past five years.

When exploring the mysteries of a fine spirit, it is tempting to start with the least expensive or youngest. This is not a good idea with cognac. A great place to begin is at the VSOP level, because here it is possible to experience the finesse of the aromas as well as the smoothness of the spirit – without spending a fortune. Even when planning to use cognac in a cocktail, mixologists say VSOP is still the best level to start with, as it melds surprisingly well with mixers and other flavourings.

VSOP cognac prices start around £30 ($45) and go up to some heights from there. Of course, VS cognac can be had for less. Most reputable brands of XO start in the neighbourhood of £60 ($100) for the top houses, while lesser-known

Even before the recent year of the dragon in Asia, Cognac Janneau had created a line of 'dragon' cognacs that have been aged 40 or more years. With each bottle encased in its own wooden crate, this line is especially attractive to Asian consumers.

(sometimes less reputable) cognac houses may price their xos considerably lower.

When looking to buy a bottle of cognac, in general, price matters. But in addition to vs, vsop and xo cognacs, there are also diverse cognacs being produced with proprietary names, and some are on the shelves for only a short time, increasing their appeal through exclusivity. Most of these special-release cognacs are fairly pricey, and what they offer – in addition to a uniquely designed label and/or bottle – is a different take on cognac in terms of aromas and flavours. One company might emphasize spicy notes while another may concentrate on blending more fruit flavours into the spirit, depending on the customer they want to attract.

In relation to drinking cognac, many people have seen the old caricature of a wealthy gentleman with his giant, after-dinner balloon glass sporting a small measure of tawny liquid at the bottom. In fact, this type of large, round-bowled glass is rapidly going out of style. It was useful 50 or 100 years ago, when houses were kept at a much cooler temperature than they are today and brandy would typically be stored in an even colder cellar. In order to liberate the delicate aromas and flavours of the cognac, people were encouraged to use the warmth of their hands to heat the liquid in the glass. As they heated, aromas were gradually released and contained for some time in the top of the balloon-shaped glass, where they could be experienced by gentle inhalation.

We no longer need to do this. In modern houses, cognac stored at room temperature starts out warm enough to drink. After the cognac is poured, the aromas are ready to be encountered by immediately inhaling at the rim of the glass. In addition, swirling the liquid around to release the aromas is not encouraged: a gentle rotary motion of the glass is all that is needed to release the delicate fragrances of a warm cognac.

The official cognac tasting glass is relatively small, with a wide middle that closes slightly at the top to cradle the aromas of the cognac for an ideal aromatic tasting experience with this spirit.

In Cognac, it has become fashionable to use glasses that are similar in size to small white wine or sherry glasses. (This is almost a return to an early style of cognac glass, which was tiny, probably crafted more for imbibing than lengthy warming and appreciation.) Aged, sipping cognac should be served in small amounts: 20–40 ml, or around 1 fl. oz.

When shopping for cognac, it is easy to see that the top four cognac houses, with 85 per cent of Cognac's production, dominate sales around the world. Most of them have large corporations behind them, providing resources for global expansion, product development, distribution and marketing. In part or in total, LVMH Moët Hennessy Louis Vuitton owns

Hennessey, Pernod Ricard owns Martell, Beam Global (now itself owned by Suntory) owns Courvoisier and Rémy Martin is owned by the Rémy Cointreau company. In March 2012 these four companies were reported to have generated around £3 billion ($5 billion) in worldwide sales during the previous year.

There are many other fine cognacs to try, depending on availability, the occasion – and one's bank balance, of course. These additional brands tend to be the most widely available: ABK6, Bache-Gabrielsen, Baron Otard, Bisquit, Camus, Conjure, De Luze, Delamain, Ferrand, François Voyer, Frapin, Gautier, Hardy, Hine, Jean Fillioux, Jenssen, Landy, Louis Royer, Meukow, Normandin-Mercier, Peyrat and Prunier.

10

Cognac Cocktails and
21st-century Trends

Luxury is the essence of cognac's image in the twenty-first century. Whether cognac is sipped straight, blended into a high-end cocktail or combined with a mixer, the people imbibing it are all pursuing a deluxe experience. In Britain, the u.s. and countries that orient themselves culturally with the West, there is still a reliable segment of the population interested in high-end brandies that are sipped neat, after dinner. Cognac's luxury lifestyle association has remained important at this level, with top-tier cognacs dominating. However, the current brandy renaissance has several trending sources: East Asian culture, American popular music and lush mixology.

Two concurrent cultures began consuming a great deal more cognac and brandy at the end of the twentieth century. One was in Asia, specifically high-end Hong Kong consumers. The other was urban (inner city) u.s. consumers. With cognac growth basically flat in most other parts of the world, cognac producers began paying much more attention to these two areas, and they have definitely reaped the rewards.

Increased urban u.s. brandy and cognac consumption occurred in locations with predominantly Hispanic and black populations. Within Latino society, this could be the result of further extension of the Spanish brandy culture

A mixologist at Cognac's Cocktail Summit creates a flamed drink for the cocktail competition.

already prevalent in Mexico and other Latin countries. Within urban black society, a number of explanations have been suggested, from rebellion and differentiation of current young people to the European experience of black servicemen in the Second World War – though the latter cause would date any increased interest in brandy pretty far back in the twentieth century. In fact, there had been considerable consumption of brandy in the inner city for several decades before the urban rap movement began to vocalize it. Much of the rest of the world only became aware of it in 2001 with Busta Rhymes's song featuring P. Diddy, 'Pass the Courvoisier', and with its subsequent (equally successful) remix and music video.

In the dozen years after that, over 150 rap songs were released containing references to cognac brands, especially Courvoisier and Hennessy (also spelled Hennessey). At the same time, to concentrate on this market, cognac producers formed partnerships with several major artists. Ludacris put out his Conjure cognac with Kim Hartmann, owner of Birkedal Hartmann cognac – though in the advertising campaign Ludacris is identified only by his real name, Chris Bridges. Dr Dre released his Aftermath cognac in conjunction with ABK6 cognac. The rapper T.I. and Martell cognac announced their affiliation – but Martell dissolved it a few months later when T.I. was sent to prison.

Cognacs have also been produced specifically for the high-end urban trade by some of the most important cognac companies. The musician Jay-Z introduced d'Ussé to the U.S.; this cognac is a product of the Bacardi Company, which also owns Baron Otard cognac. Rémy Martin recently had a limited release of a VSOP cognac called Urban Lights, with a label design that glowed red in ultraviolet light. And there are more each year. It is interesting to note that on their websites cognac companies do not always list these products, preferring that consumers visit the websites with the proprietary names of the particular cognacs. At this point in time, cognac producers seem to be following several different paths simultaneously in their quest to sustain the global luxury appeal of this classic spirit.

Turning to Asia, there is only one word for cognac consumption: explosive. Though many people have heard that top Bordeaux wines are now requisite accessories for the high-end Chinese consumer, not everyone knows that cognac is now the Bordeaux equivalent in spirits. Whereas Japanese customers prefer Scotch whisky as their favourite Western spirit, the Chinese and other Asians are fervent consumers of brandies, and in China that means XO, Extra and Vintage: only top of the line will do. The older and rarer, the better.

In 2012 the Chinese market for cognac outstripped the erstwhile number-one market, the United States, in value. Due to this gargantuan growth rate, much of the focus of cognac's producers has been on Asia for the past few years. And because the Chinese tend to buy only the top of the line, this situation is expected to continue for the foreseeable future. A sizeable number of cognac houses is producing special bottlings, blends and labels for the Chinese market – whether or not this is something they publicize in the rest of the world.

Recently, articles in the press have questioned whether cognac can continue to satisfy Chinese demand. Savvy importers and consumers in China have also discovered armagnac, to the Armagnac region's great delight. Armagnac's noble brandies were second-in-line for centuries due to its land-locked location, but that obstacle has been overcome by modern transportation. Armagnac now basks in well-deserved prestige in China.

But the Chinese are reaching even further now, to additional markets that make authentic (grape-wine-based) brandies, the closest being Australia. For new markets, sourcing brandy from areas other than Cognac is fairly simple because most brandy producers around the world label their brandies in the same way: 3-star or vs is generally the first level, vsop the second level, and xo the third. In addition, terms like Napoléon, Extra Old and Vintage are used there, as well as proprietary names for special releases. Though the brandies in each category are not uniformly aged across the world, this labelling makes it easier for new distributors and consumers to get their start in the brandy world.

Other Asian countries are going along for the ride, too. In some, their brandy customs began with early colonial influence. In others it has come straight from urban life as seen in music videos – which is the case among young people in the Philippines today. However, other generations in this country have also maintained a tradition of consuming Spanish brandy, a favourite being Pedro Domecq's brandy de Jerez, Fundador.

There is a certain amount of cognac imported into Asian countries other than China. Vietnam, for instance, was the fifth-largest brandy consumer in the late 1990s, and its brandy consumption remains strong today. Brandy drinkers have mainly been men in the 20–50 age range, with their preferred spirit being cognac; other brandies are chosen by less than 10 per cent of these males, with about 1 per cent favouring armagnac. Top cognac houses are preferred, since much of this spirit is consumed publicly by young men in venues like nightclubs.

Brandies are also being produced in Russia and in other Asian countries. However, many of these are not actually grape wine distillations, as there are not many grapes grown in some of these regions. Brandy is big in Malaysia – in fact the biggest brandy brand in the world is Malaysia's Emperador. But the key here is what is *not* said: what the brandy is made from. Only sometimes is it made from grapes, and in those cases only sometimes are the grapes wine grapes (as opposed to table grapes).

However, there is a trend towards authenticity in certain markets. Russia's Fanagoriysky now emphasizes the oak ageing of its brandies, as do many other brandy producers on this continent. Fanagoriysky recently opened its own modern cooperage. Russia's KIN Group owns the Domaine des Broix in Cognac, from which they import distilled spirits and aged cognac. KIN also makes domestically produced, blended brandies. India's Morpheus uses some grapes grown in India and some imported from France. China is making attempts at traditional-style brandy distilling, according to a consultant who works there.

In various places, 'brandy' is simply a label on a bottle of a coloured distillation of whatever agricultural product it makes sense to use there – even pineapple. The advantage is the lower cost for the producer, as well as the customer; these brandies sell for less than half the prices of the imported brandies and cognacs.

In terms of brandy products, there is one more curious trend to mention, which seems to be happening everywhere from Armagnac to California: 'white' brandy. In the spirits industry 'white' actually refers to clear spirits. For brandy, this would seem to be a contradiction in terms, as brandies are known for their wood ageing which imparts wonderful aromas, flavours and colours to the spirit. White brandies can appear clear because they are unaged, or because they have had the wood tint filtered out.

White brandies are also native to Armagnac – in fact, their traditional 'blanche' received its official AOC (Appellation d'Origine Contrôlée) title in 2005. Blanche must be made from designated vineyard parcels, from the grapes Folle Blanche, Ugni Blanc, Baco and Colombard. Early distillation is required, followed by a three-month settling or 'maturation' period. Then a producer can begin adding water to the high-alcohol spirit to bring it down to its bottling level of around 40 per cent. In practice, this phase usually takes place over a period longer than three months.

White brandies capitalize on the fashion for clear spirit bases for cocktails, a trend with notable growth the last few decades which does not seem to be abating. The white brandy fashion is visible even in cognac. In 2010 Rémy Martin produced a clear 'V' unaged spirit from cognac. Hennessy, which also has a Black cognac, did a 'Pure White', which was tested in several countries. Technically these cannot be called 'cognac' because cognac requires barrel-ageing for a specified time. But more white brandies will probably be available soon, in part because this could be a way to sell brandy from the Cognac region without waiting the many years required for ageing traditional styles.

In other areas, South Africa's Collison's makes a White Gold brandy. In the u.s., Christian Brothers has jumped into the ring with its 'Frost' brandy. This is aged in oak, but then processed (and flavoured, in this case) so it appears clear in the bottle. For all these clear spirits, the recommendations are to drink them chilled – perhaps as an alternative to vodka in cocktails for the fashionable mixology trend. And it is in the mixology arena that cognac is really getting hot.

11
Small-batch Brandies and Cognacs

Even before the cocktail culture began revitalizing cognac early in the twenty-first century, there were stirrings of brandy's revival around the globe, particularly in the u.s. where, in the 1980s, the artisan spirit movement encouraged new brandy producers to get into the game. But of the two most famous new producers, one has become a staple of artisan brandy in the u.s., and one has disappeared.

Cognac's illustrious Rémy Martin cognac company formed a partnership with Jack Davies of California's Napa sparkling winery Schramsberg Vineyards in 1982. They established a distillery in the Carneros wine region that straddles Napa and Sonoma. It was called RMS, and great things were expected. But rather than being lauded for their authentically cognac-styled brandy, RMS received little attention from American customers – even when they later changed their name to Carneros Alambic.

Also during the early 1980s, the distillery Germain-Robin was founded in California's remote, wooded, northern county of Mendocino, by the American Ansley Coale and Cognac native Hubert Germain-Robin. Again, there was little excitement in the u.s., though the brandies received consistently great reviews. Both companies persevered for more than

When a Californian and a Frenchman pooled their resources in the late 20th century to establish the Germain-Robin brandy production company in Northern California, they began with an unassuming yet distinguished bottle for their product.

fifteen years. But by the late 1990s, RMS/Carneros Alambic had folded, while Germain-Robin had finally turned a profit and has continued producing artisanal spirits to this day.

Coale and Germain-Robin instituted a new approach to selecting grapes for their brandies. At first they sourced the same grape varieties that are used in Cognac. But Coale and Germain-Robin discovered that the brandy made in Mendocino, California, did not have the taste they were after, because the grapes were not grown on Cognac's chalky soil. Realizing they were in the midst of excellent wine grape country, they decided to take a chance and experiment with making their brandies out of the best local grapes. After exhaustive trials they eventually discovered how to make fine-quality brandy with these grapes – though Coale and Germain-Robin did have to persuade the farmers they contracted with to pick a little earlier to maintain the acidity balance their brandy needed. Now Germain-Robin uses one cognac grape, Colombard, but relies mainly on Pinot Noir. Depending on the harvest, they also include locally grown grapes such as Sémillon, Sauvignon Blanc, Zinfandel, Chenin Blanc and Muscat in their brandies.

Once they had chosen the best ingredients, Coale found that he had to educate the public about the contents of his brandies. He observed that Americans looked at brandy as a kind of static commodity: they bought by brand name and moved up by price, not really aware of what went into the brandies. Slowly, Coale has been taking the American public along a learning curve.

After his success in Mendocino, the distiller Hubert Germain-Robin has gone on to consult with brandy producers in Asia and other parts of the world. Because of the popularity of cognac and brandy today, many companies are eager to become brandy distillers. But not all of them have good grapes to distil with – and some don't even have grapes – so Hubert often finds himself in the midst of a fascinating exploration of this brave new world.

Back in the U.S., a few other producers had decided to jump into the game. Daniel Farber of Osocalis in the Santa Cruz area of California calls himself 'generation 1.5' of California brandy. Before establishing Osocalis, he travelled to France and Spain to learn about brandy production and ageing.

At California's Germain-Robin brandy company, it didn't hurt that the master distiller had a wonderfully brooding look and a double-barrelled French name.

When he started distilling later in the 1980s, he was not aware of the new RMS and Germain-Robin distilleries; he simply wanted to produce a world-class brandy. Now, he credits Hubert Germain-Robin with being a visionary and pioneer in creating the 'California alembic' style of brandy.

Farber uses cognac-type distillation and California grapes such as Pinot Noir, Sémillon and Colombard; every year the blend is a little different. Stylistically, Farber believes Osocalis brandies are a cross between armagnac and cognac. He tried ageing his brandies in American oak, but realized French Limousin oak was far better. Though he usually releases each vintage when it has aged (and doesn't generally blend them), he is enthralled by the notion that a brandy and a human have roughly the same age span: up to 80 years.

Jepson is another California brandy that began in Mendocino. Bob Jepson bought a property near the Russian River in 1985 to establish a distillery and winery there. The current owners took it over in 2009 and named it Jaxon Keys Winery and Distillery. Under the Jepson name they still produce brandy that is distilled on the property and made from the Colombard grown in their vineyards.

Back in the Carneros region, when the Etude winery took over the former Carneros Alambic property (originally RMS) in 2002, they also acquired brandy that was ageing there in casks. The company now sells an expensive Etude XO brandy – aged twenty years and blended by their winemaker – which was made from locally grown grapes: Pinot Noir, Colombard, Chenin Blanc, Palomino, Chardonnay, Ugni Blanc, Muscat and Folle Blanche.

Another distillery that started as a small artisanal venture is Charbay, which boasts a thirteenth-generation distiller whose father immigrated from the Balkans in 1962. This family enterprise began in 1983 on Spring Mountain, part of the range that divides the Napa and Sonoma wine regions. After great success with their vodkas, the Karakasevic family branched out and a few years ago they released their Brandy No. 83, made from Folle Blanche grapes – a spirit which they had been aging for 27 years.

Undoubtedly, even as this chapter is being read, small distillers in various parts of the country are starting up new brandy ventures. One of the most recent is Finger Lakes Distilling in rural upstate New York, which is owned by Brian McKenzie. He also began by producing other grape-based spirits, as his distillery is located in the middle of the Finger Lakes wine region. McKenzie is especially interested in brandy because so few artisan producers are making it. He distilled the brandy soon after the company started up a few years ago. The first batch was released in 2012 when it had aged to his satisfaction; it was made with local grapes including Gewürztraminer and other native and hybrid varieties.

Another notable young distiller, Emmanuel Painturaud, is located in Cognac itself. He is part of a small, intriguing initiative spearheaded by a small number of families who have been growing grapes and making wine to supply the large cognac houses. But as of a few years ago, a tiny percentage of grape growers in Cognac has begun to take on the extra financial risk of ageing, labelling and marketing their own cognacs. They are hoping that with an increased interest in cognac and in all things artisanal, the public will be receptive to a family-made cognac. This movement mirrors the initiative of the 'grower-producers' of the Champagne region, who began receiving outside attention – and great reviews – just about the turn of the twenty-first century, and are now a great success.

Emmanuel works with his father and brother on a small farm where his grandfather first had a modest still in 1934. They grow grapes, make wine, and distil and sell some to

Rémy Martin, which requires them to distil wine on the lees for 'a rounder, deeper richer flavour'. And they are proud of the product they supply to this large company. But now, Emmanuel also takes some of his own wine and distils it to make his own artisanal cognacs.

The Painturaud family uses their older barrels for ageing and storing the cognacs they blend for themselves. They buy four or five of the very expensive new barrels a year. These can be considered 'new' for the three years, which means that they can be used for the critical first six months of cognac ageing. The Painturauds blend three or four cognacs together to make their final blend of each style of cognac. In the past, the family aged and bottled a small amount for themselves. Now they are bottling to sell, so they make several different styles. Before Emmanuel came back to the family business, the

In Cognac, barrels of ageing cognacs are sampled periodically with the traditional glass 'wine thief' tool. This sample in a shaft of sunlight is in the perfect position to be judged on its taste, aroma and appearance for the Palazzi company.

Nicolas Palazzi has recently come on the scene in Cognac with excellent contacts that supply the ingredients for his discerning customers worldwide. Here, a custom blend is being hand-bottled for private consumption.

Painturauds did not make an xo, but today they do because it is in demand.

There are about 1,000 family-owned operations in Cognac, but this number is decreasing as the adult children do not want to remain out in the countryside, working the land. While there are other young people who might want to start a small business of growing and distilling in Cognac, unfortunately they usually cannot afford it. Emmanuel blames this on the increase in land prices; he maintains that in the past five years vineyard prices have become nearly prohibitive in all areas of Cognac due to an enormous increase in demand fuelled by Chinese high-end customers and American rap musicians.

Another way family-aged cognacs come on the market is through a company like PM Spirits, owned by Nicolas Palazzi, who now lives in New York. Raised by his grandparents in Bordeaux, Palazzi established a custom, small-batch cognac business in 2008. Beginning with the cognac that a friend of his grandfather wanted to sell, Palazzi was soon referred to others in similar situations. Perhaps that family was getting out of the cognac business; perhaps they needed money; perhaps they simply wanted to take advantage of the current popularity of cognac around the world. Whatever the reason, Palazzi has been able to source aged cognacs, which he collects – and ages further, if necessary – then bottles and sells to elite customers in New York and other cities.

Palazzi also takes this one step further: he will custom-blend and custom-bottle cognac for individuals who desire their own distinctive cognac. After numerous careful, detailed tastings with a customer (at home or in Cognac) Palazzi works to design labels and distinctive hand-blown bottles for these unique blends of cognac, which are supplied to collectors and for special events.

There's a popular song called 'Everything Old is New Again' – and there is no truer place to apply this phrase than to the world of brandy today.

Recipes

Here are some of the most famous cocktail recipes that use cognac or brandy as their base spirit – and some new ones. Classics may have different proportions than the present-day cocktail imbiber is used to. Some classic cocktails are modernized here with slight variations, such as using brandy de Jerez instead of cognac. Cocktail connoisseurs will relish the opportunity to widen their realm of experience by tasting these cocktails.

Brandy Alexander

This is the first drink anyone mentions when asked for the name of a cocktail made with brandy. But nowadays few of us know what it is – except for mixologists, of course. From the 1930s to the 1970s, this was a very popular drink in the u.s., with some geographical differences: in the south, brandy was a man's drink, while in the north the frothiness of this cocktail made it more of a ladies' drink. This recipe comes from E. & J. Gallo, who would have produced the brandy used for many of these cocktails made in America during the mid-twentieth century.

30 ml (1 fl. oz) brandy
30 ml (1 fl. oz) cream
30 ml (1 fl. oz) dark crème de cacao
ground nutmeg

Shake liquid ingredients well with ice. Strain into a cocktail glass and dust with ground nutmeg.

Brandy Collins

One of the newer bodegas in Jerez is, ironically, called Bodegas Tradición. They source older brandies from around the region, then age and blend them before bottling. As a young company, they are open to new styles of cocktails with old brandies. Here is a recipe for a 'Collins' made with brandy de Jerez.

50 ml brandy de Jerez
30 ml fresh lemon juice
20 ml simple syrup
iced soda water
slice lemon

Mix all ingredients but the soda water with ice. Blend in a shaker, strain into a Collins glass filled with ice. Top with soda water, garnish with a lemon slice and serve with a straw.

Brandy Crusta

This is a recipe made for me by Alexandre Lambert, bartender at Bar Louise in the Hôtel François Premier, which opened in 2012 in the centre of the city of Cognac. The cocktail is based on the original created by Joseph Santini at his bar The Jewel of the South in New Orleans in the mid-nineteenth century. Lambert says Hennessy's Fine de Cognac is a cross between a VS and VSOP; he also recommends using VSOP cognac for this drink.

1 dash Peychaud's Bitters
1 dash Angostura bitters
1 tsp original recipe triple sec
1 tsp Luxardo Maraschino liqueur
40 ml Hennessy 'Fine de Cognac'
2 tsp fresh lemon juice

1 tsp simple syrup
granulated sugar
lemon peel

Stir ice cubes in a glass jug. Add liquid ingredients and continue stirring until blended. Strain into a coupe glass rimmed with granulated sugar. Drop in a thin spiral of lemon peel.

Cognac Punch

The British created punch using brandy, the word 'punch' coming from the Hindi word for five, the number of ingredients used: sugar, brandy, lemon or lime juice, water and flavourings. Wine was sometimes used in place of, or in addition to, water. This recipe is from the Cognac Bureau (BNIC) in France.

peel of 4 lemons
250 g (9 oz) icing (superfine) sugar
250 ml (1 cup) fresh lemon juice, strained
750 ml (1 bottle, or 3 cups) VSOP (or VS) cognac
250 ml (1 cup) rum
1.5 l (6 cups) cold water
1 whole nutmeg

Muddle the lemon peels with the sugar and let sit for at least 1 hour. Muddle again and add the lemon juice, stirring until sugar has dissolved. Strain out the lemon peels. Add the cognac and the rum and stir. Refrigerate.

To serve, pour into a punchbowl filled halfway with ice cubes, add the cold water and stir. Grate 1/2 nutmeg over the top.

Cognac Long Drink

Visitors to Cognac in the summer are first surprised to see precious cognac diluted with soda or tonic. Once they have one in hand, they get it. The Cognac Long Drink is always in fashion during Cognac's hottest days and nights. For a simple 'long-drink', vs is generally used – but vsop is even better. This recipe is from the BNIC.

30 ml (1 fl. oz) cognac
90 ml (3 fl. oz) tonic water

Pour into in a Collins glass containing ice cubes. Stir lightly.

French Connection

An after-dinner drink, with the amaretto not-so-subtly flavouring the cognac. It's also possible to adjust the proportions to taste, so that there is half as much amaretto as cognac.

30 ml (1 fl. oz) cognac
30 ml (1 fl. oz) amaretto liqueur

Pour over ice cubes in a highball glass and stir until blended.

Horse's Neck

A classic drink to sip on a warm evening while wandering through the Cognac Blues Passion, an incredible outdoor music festival held every July in a park in the centre of the town of Cognac. Here is the way it should be served, according to the BNIC.

30 ml (1 fl. oz) cognac, vs or vsop
dash Angostura bitters
ginger ale
orange peel (optional)

Pour cognac over a couple of ice cubes in a Collins glass. Add a dash of bitters. Top up with ginger ale. Optional: add a thin twist of orange peel to decorate.

Hot Toddy

Essentially, this is lemony hot water sweetened with honey, with a 'medicinal' dose of brandy. For a little more flavour, make it with tea instead of hot water. Either way, people have been drinking this for centuries to ward off chills and colds.

1 tbsp honey
2 tsp lemon juice
125 ml (½ cup) very hot water
30 ml (1 fl. oz) brandy

Combine honey, lemon juice and hot water in a mug. Stir in brandy just before serving.

Medicinal Brandy

This can be given in the case of colds or scratchy throats. In the past it was also considered suitable for invalids or those recovering from an illness because the milk provides nourishment. It is traditional in Italy, as well as many other countries.

180 ml (6 fl. oz) milk
30 ml (1 fl. oz) brandy
1 tsp sugar (optional)

Heat milk to just below boiling – or use an espresso machine or frothing device to foam the milk. Pour into a glass or mug. Stir in brandy. Sweeten with sugar if desired. Serve either morning or night.

Modern Mojito

A recipe from Spain, from Pedro Domecq, makers of brandy de Jerez. This is an informal use for a traditional brandy, the favourite of one of the employees there. It was provided with no specific amounts; this recipe was derived by testing various combinations of the ingredients. It is meant to be a fresh and healthy drink, so feel free to add more mint leaves and lemon juice.

fresh mint leaves
2 tsp sugar
1 tbsp fresh lemon juice
50 ml brandy de Jerez
crushed ice

Muddle the mint leaves and sugar in a shaker. Add lemon and brandy and shake well, until sugar has dissolved. Pour into a Manhattan glass half-filled with crushed ice.

Pisco Punch

The original recipe – made by dedicated mixologists today – contains a syrup made from gum arabic from the acacia tree. There's a lengthy process involved in combining the gum arabic with a sugar solution, but mixologists swear it's worth it. The recipe below, provided by Pisco Portón from Peru, is a simplified version, easier for home entertaining.

1 fresh pineapple
235 ml (1 cup) simple syrup
470 ml (2 cups) bottled water
750 ml (1 bottle, or 3 cups) Pisco Portón
300 ml (1 ¼ cups) fresh lemon juice

Cut a fresh pineapple in pieces about 1.5 by 4 cm (0.5 by 1.5 in.) and soak overnight in simple syrup. In the morning, mix the rest of the ingredients in a big bowl. Lemon juice or simple syrup may be added to taste. Use around 100 ml (3–4 fl. oz) of punch per glass, adding a cube of the soaked pineapple to each.

Pisco Sour

When there's a party in Peru, people expect Pisco Sours. According to the sisters who created Macchu Pisco, here's how they do it:

2 parts Peruvian pisco (preferably Quebranta-grape pisco)
1 part fresh lime juice
1 part sugar
1 shot of egg white
Angostura bitters
ice

Put the first four ingredients in a blender with two cups of ice. Blend well. Pour into a chilled glass. Top each cocktail with a few drops of Angostura bitters. Number of servings? Your call . . .

Sidecar

From the BNIC, this recipe begins with a great history of the drink by the mixologist Dale DeGroff:

The Sidecar is our legacy from the Crusta, although the twentieth century chapter to the story is poorly documented. Harry's New York Bar claims credit for the Sidecar. But Colin Field, the head bartender at the Ritz Hotel's Hemingway Bar in Paris, is convinced his predecessor Frank Meier, Hemingway's legendary barman in the early days of the Ritz, created the drink sometime in 1923 although there is no documentation to prove his claim. The single bit of evidence we have in print is the 1922 book by Robert Vermeire of the Embassy bar in London called 'Cocktails: How to Mix Them'. In it, the drink is credited to a barman named MacGarry at the Bucks Club in London.

45 ml (1½ fl. oz) VSOP cognac
30 ml (1 fl. oz) triple sec
20 ml (¾ fl. oz) fresh lemon juice
orange zest (optional)

Combine all ingredients in a mixing glass and strain into a small cocktail glass with a lightly sugared rim. Garnish with a small flamed orange zest.

Stinger

This cocktail was a classic for many years, though it may not be the first on everyone's list today. The name probably refers to the 'zing' you get with this drink. According to personal preference, the amount of crème de menthe may be decreased; some people like the proportions of two parts brandy to one part crème de menthe.

30 ml (1 fl. oz) brandy
30 ml (1 fl. oz) crème de menthe
crushed ice
fresh mint leaf (optional)

Put in a shaker with crushed ice and shake until blended. Strain into a cocktail glass. Garnish with fresh mint leaf if desired.

Summit Cocktail

A few years ago, when the BNIC began encouraging bartenders to experiment with cognac in cocktails, they held a Cocktail Summit and invited numerous celebrated mixologists. This cocktail was created for the event by Andy Seymour and is now a new classic, served at many Cognac Bureau occasions around the world.

zest of 1 lime
4 thin slices fresh ginger
45 ml (1½ fl. oz) VSOP cognac
60 ml (2 fl. oz) lemon and lime soda
1 long piece cucumber

Put lime and ginger into a glass, pour in half the cognac, press lightly 2–3 times. Half fill with ice, stir for 5 seconds. Pour in remaining cognac. Add lemon and lime soda and cucumber, stir well and serve immediately.

Suprème de l'Armagnac

This cocktail was recently developed by Philippe Olivier, head barman at the Hôtel de Crillon in Paris, working with the Armagnac Bureau (BNIA). It melds citrus and brandy, which is a classic flavour combination that works for many palates around the world.

40 ml (1¼ fl. oz) armagnac
30 ml (1 fl. oz) grapefruit juice
2 tsp orange juice pressed from peeled orange segments
maraschino cherry (optional)

Shake all ingredients together well over ice. Strain into cocktail glass. Optional: garnish rim with a maraschino cherry.

Select Bibliography

Calabrese, Salvatore, *Cognac: A Liquid History* (London, 2005)

'Clem Hill Tell Test History', *Daily News*, Perth (11 March 1933), from http://nla.gov.au

Cullen, L. M, *The Brandy Trade under the Ancien Régime: Regional Specialisation in the Charente* (Cambridge, 1998)

Dicum, Gregory, *The Pisco Book* (San Francisco, 2011)

Faith, Nicholas, *Cognac* (Boston, 1987)

Fromm, Alfred, *Marketing California Wine and Brandy: Oral History Transcript*, ed. Ruth Teiser, Regional Oral History Office, The Bancroft Library, University of California at Berkeley (1984)

Jarrard, Kyle, *Cognac: The Seductive Saga of the World's Most Coveted Spirit* (Hoboken, NJ, 2005)

Kops, Henriette de Bruyn, *A Spirited Exchange: The Wine and Brandy Trade between France and the Dutch Republic in its Atlantic Framework, 1600–1650* (Boston, 2007)

Miller, Anistatia, and Jared Brown, *A Spirituous Journey: A History of Drink, Book One – From the Birth of Spirits to the Birth of the Cocktail* (Cheltenham, 2009)

——, *A Spirituous Journey: A History of Drink, Book Two – From the Publicans to Master Mixologists* (Cheltenham, 2010)

Neal, Charles, *Armagnac: The Definitive Guide to France's Premier Brandy* (San Francisco, 1998)

Wilson, C. Anne, *Water of Life: A History of Wine-Distilling and Spirits 500 BC–AD 2000* (Totnes, Devon, 2006)

Websites and Associations

Brandy Producers

Asbach Brandy
www.asbach.de

Beam
www.beamglobal.com

Birkedal Hartmann
www.birkedal-hartmann.com

The Blanche
www.theblanche.com

The Christian Brothers
www.christianbrothersbrandy.com

E&J Brandy
www.ejbrandy.com

Etude
www.etudewines.com

Finger Lakes Distilling
www.fingerlakesdistilling.com

Hine
www.hinecognac.com

Jaxon Keys Winery and Distillery
www.jaxonkeys.com

Korbel
www.korbelbrandy.com

PM Spirits
www.pmspirits.com

Proshyan
www.proshyan.am

Romate
wwww.romate.com

Brandy Information

All About Brandy, Cognac and Armagnac
www.tastings.com/spirits/brandy

The American Distilling Institute
www.distilling.com

Armagnac: The True Spirit of France
www.armagnac.fr

Beverage Media Group
www.bevnetwork.com

Brandy de Jerez
www.brandydejerez.es

Bureau National Interprofessionel de Cognac
www.cognac.fr/cognac

Cognac Expert
www.cognac-expert.com

Drinks International
www.drinksint.com

Experience Cognac
www.experience-cognac.fr

International Bartenders Association
www.iba-world.com

Paul Masson Winery Operations and Management, 1944–1988
http://archive.org

Pisco Chile
www.piscochile.com

Derek, Ramsden, *South African Brandy in an International Context*,
Dissertation, 2012
www.capewineacademy.co.za

Rap Genius
www.rapgenius.com

Gary, Regan, 'Behind the Drink: The Brandy Alexander'
http://liquor.com

Shanken News Daily
www.shankennewsdaily.com

South Africa Brandy Foundation
www.sabrandy.co.za

Acknowledgements

In Armenia: Ararat/Pernod-Ricard, Noy, Proshyan Brandy, Vedi-Alco; in Armagnac: Amanda Garnham, the BNIA and all its members, Ithier Bouchard at Tariquet, Jean Castarède, Arnaud and Denis Lesgourgues at Château de Laubade; in Australia Matt Redin at Angove, Rob Hirst at Fine Wine Partners, John Geber and Marty Powell at Château Tanunda, in Cognac: Jean-Louis Carbonnier, Nicki Sizemore and the BNIC and all its members; in Georgia: Tina Kezeli and Georgie Apkhazava of the Georgian Wine Association Ekaterine Egutia, Zviad Kvlividze, David Abzianidze and Sarajishvili, Tfilisi Marani, Kakheti Traditional Winemaking; in Jerez: Beam Domecq, Carmen Aumesquet and Cesar Saldaña at Consejo Regulador del Brandy de Jerez, Bodegas Fernando de Castilla, González Byass, Sánchez Romate, Lorenzo Garcia-Iglesias at Bodegas Tradición; for pisco, Elizabeth and Melanie Asher at Macchu Pisco, Johnny Schuler at Pisco Portón, Guillermo L. Toro-Lira; in South Africa: Louise and Tessa de Kock, Elsa Vogts KWV; in the U.S., Bill Owens at the American Distilling Institute, Scott DiSalvo and Russell Ricketts at E&J Gallo, Brian McKenzie at Finger Lakes Distilling, Ansley Coale, Hubert Germain-Robin, Dan Farber at Osocalis.

Additionally: David Baker, Tim Clarke, Concord Writers Group, Jill and Dale DeGroff, Pierluigi Donini, Branko Gerovac, Kyle Jarrard, Lauren Kinelski at RemyUSA, Sandra MacDonald, Charles de Bournet Marnier Lapostolle Maria Mata at Mascaro, Elizabeth Minchilli, Mark Pallot at Beam Global, Norm Roby, Ken Simonson,

Hamish Smith, Jan Solomon, Calvin Stovall, Ann Tuennerman at
Tales of the Cocktail, Elisa Vignuda and Kirsten Amann at Fratelli
Branca, Rosie Vidal, David Wondrich.

Photo Acknowledgements

The author and the publishers wish to express their thanks to the below sources of illustrative material and/or permission to reproduce it.

Courtesy of Angove: pp. 86, 87; Courtesy of Armagnac Delord: pp. 46, 47 top, 51 top, 52; Bigstock: p. 6 (Marco Mayer); © BNIC: pp. 10, 105 (Roger Cantagrel), 23, 36, 111 (Gérard Martron), 30, 39 (Bernard Verrax), 101 (Jean-Yves Boyer), 108 (Stéphane Carbeau); Bureau National Interprofessional de l'Armagnac (BNIA): p. 27; Courtesy of Chateau de L'Aubade: pp. 42, 43, 44, 46, 47, 48–9, 51, 52 (Michael Carossio); Courtesy of Chateau Tanunda: p. 84; Courtesy of Chateau du Tariquet: pp. 42, 44; Courtesy of Cognac Hardy: p. 12; Courtesy of E&J Gallo: p. 94; Becky Sue Epstein: pp. 61, 79; Branko Gerovac: pp. 56, 57, 59, 60, 61, 63, 64, 67 bottom; Courtesy of Germain-Robin: pp. 118, 120; Courtesy of Gonzalez-Byass: p. 28; Courtesy of Janneau: p. 106; Courtesy of Korbel Brandy: pp. 94, 95, 96, 97; Courtesy of Nicolas Palazzi: pp. 123, 124; Courtesy of Sànchez Romate: pp. 48–9, 70–71, 72–3, 75; Courtesy of Sarajishvili: pp. 65, 66, 67 top; U.S. National Library of Medicine, Bethesda, Maryland: p. 14; image supplied by Van Ryn's: p. 88.

Index

italic numbers refer to illustrations; **bold** to recipes